If You Think You Can, **YOU** Can

Stop Doubting, Stop Worrying, and Start BELIEVING!

DONA M. DEANE

If You Think You Can, YOU Can

Stop Doubting, Stop Worrying, and Start BELIEVING!

Copyright © 2018 Dona M. Deane

For further information, you can contact the author via:

Website: www.donamdeane.com

Twitter: www.twitter.com/donadeane

LinkedIn: www.linkedin.com/donadeane

ISBN 978-0-9958995-2-0 (eBook)

ISBN 978-0-9958995-3-7 (Paperback)

DEDICATION

To my mom who continues to inspire me with her love, kindness, courage, and wisdom. Mom, words cannot adequately express how happy and grateful I am that you're my mother and my children's grandmother. You are my ultimate hero! Your support over the years has been incredible, and I cannot ever thank you enough!

And to my Aunt Elaine, who passed on during the writing of this book. You are gone, but you will remain in my heart forever. Your sudden passing reminded me of just how precious life is. I will always cherish the special moments we shared together.

Rest peacefully, my dear auntie!

And finally to my grandmother, Inez (Aundine) Marshall, who is also gone but not forgotten. Thank you for teaching me to be kind, humble, graceful, and grateful even during difficult times. Because of you, rather than being served, I've learned to be of service to others.

Also by Dona M. Deane

It's All Up to YOU

Table of Contents

INTRODUCTION

Have no fear of moving into the unknown. Simply step out fearlessly knowing that I am with you, therefore no harm can befall you; all is very, very well. Do this in complete faith and confidence.

- POPE JOHN PAUL II -

* * *

One of my favorite quotes by author and motivational speaker Les Brown says: *If you do what is easy, your life will be hard. If you do what is hard, your life will be easy.*

This quote seems simple, and it makes perfect sense. It's natural for us to look for "easy" when we're trying to pursue a dream or an opportunity or when we find ourselves in a situation or a predicament, even when those things aren't going to move us much further along on our life's journey.

It is true that if we want a different outcome we must do things differently. Sometimes, we cannot make significant progress until something happens that will compel us to make the changes we wish to see.

So, as I stood looking out my living room window on a snowy afternoon thinking those thoughts—torn between wanting to focus on my chores at hand and the urge to keep writing—my thoughts grew deeper. I reflected on the changes that I'd decided to make in my life the year prior—changes that required me to put my priorities in order. I had to learn how to say *no*, with no guilt, apologies, or excuses to certain people and things that weren't moving me forward.

I decided that I'd start saying no because I felt that I was being pulled in a gazillion different directions and wanted to save my yeses for more important things, people, and events. More importantly, I desperately wanted to focus on me—my needs, dreams, and goals. *I wanted to give top priority to the "one thing" that was tugging at my heart and mind—that thing that I've been passionate about for quite some time, and that is my writing.*

I had discovered a long time ago that I was passionate about writing and wanted to do so in a meaningful way, but the busyness of life would often get in the way. However, this time I decided to stay focused on my vision, no matter what, and in doing so, I was able to write and publish two books within one year while still juggling work and family life.

For me to accomplish my writing goal meant that I also had to stand firmly on my noes even when I *really, really* wanted to say yes. It is hard to say no to the people who you care about. My thinking is that since I need to focus on making changes that could benefit those around me, it would be better for me to stand strong. We all have to make personal sacrifices at some point or another; I say it's better to do "it" sooner rather than later.

I also gave up on my wish to win the best housekeeping award. *Hello!* It finally dawned on me that if I hadn't won one after all these years of working so hard to try and earn one, then it's more than likely I won't ever win one. There have been many times in the past when I was sure I could compete with Martha Stewart and win an award hands down. Well, perhaps I'm pushing this a bit too far because I don't know of anyone who would be brave enough to want to stand toe to toe with Ms. Martha.

For you to fully understand where I'm coming from, you would have had to know who I was, say, some fifteen or twenty years ago. Just to give you an idea, I was the girl who had to have all her life's goals planned out and her surroundings kept in a neat and orderly manner—no chaos or drama was allowed in my life.

Fast forward a bit, and oh boy, has my life changed! Lately, I've been saying "life happens" when I am referring to the changes that may occur in one's life cycle. To better explain, I wrote in my previous book, *It's All Up to YOU: Strive to Feel Better, Do Better, and Live Better* that as we grow older, somewhere along the way life happens: we go to college, and before we have a chance to graduate, we're already in debt. We move on to get a job, buy a car or a house, or both. We get married, have kids, and get into more debt, and these situations cause our dreams to get delayed or, plainly put, we didn't get anywhere close to what we'd envisioned.

On the flip side, the worse could occur, we may lose our jobs, businesses, or homes, get a divorce, lose a loved one, get sad and lonely, and/or sink further into debt, and there we go. Life goes on in any case. Well, at least we hope that life goes on. The sad situation is that many people give up on life way too soon because they lose faith; they don't realize that although their lives might be different after a change that it is still possible to move forward to create a rewarding and satisfying life.

You could say that I experienced many of the changes listed above. That afternoon, as I stood looking out my window, I noticed the trees that had lost their leaves and the yellow and brown vista that was lush green with bountiful blooms of flowers just a couple of months before, and I thought of many people who have inspired me over the years. People like Oprah Winfrey, J.K. Rowling, Sir Richard Branson, Dwayne (The Rock) Johnson, Shonda Rhimes, Steve Harvey, Tyler Perry, and my own mother have been sources of inspiration.

My mother has made many personal sacrifices to become the woman she is today. She is my ultimate hero.

I also thought of others who have gone on before us like Abraham Lincoln, Albert Einstein, Thomas Edison, Nelson Mandela, Maya Angelou, and many other extraordinary people who might have hesitated or doubted their abilities to do what they believed they could, but in any case, they took the leap of faith and pursued their vision.

What did it take for them to move forward from the pain of a betrayal, disappointment, setback, or a loss? How did they navigate their way to become strong, confident, and highly successful people—to the point where they're able to live a life of clarity? **It's evident that these people were passionate, but more importantly they knew they had a purpose to fulfill.** I believe this is what many of us desire—a life where we know clearly what we need to do and aim steadfastly in that direction. A life where we can choose to stand on the truth, even if it means that we stand alone. A life where we can freely say yes to other people and opportunities without hesitating or worrying about whether we'll be judged or criticized. A life where we can walk or stand on our stories instead of dwelling on them. A life where we can live with a real sense of abundance—where we can feel free to be who we were created to be.

I recalled a YouTube video where Les said that before he became a motivational speaker he'd sit in the audience watching and listening to people like Tony Robbins speak, thinking "I can do that," but as soon as he got to the parking lot he'd begin to doubt his abilities.

Many of us have been there—at a certain point in our lives, where we find ourselves questioning our ideas or our capabilities when confronted with doing the very things we know deep down we ought to be doing—things that could positively impact our lives.

Now, let me stop for a moment and ask you this question: Have you ever had moments when you realize that you should be focusing all your time, effort, and resources into getting something done, but you don't? Instead, you hesitate or procrastinate. And, what about that feeling that you get deep down inside, when you want to offer your input or strongly disagree with someone about something you know could make a significant difference, but you didn't? Still to this day, you wish you had said or done something.

Can you recall an incident as I've described above? If you can, did you hold back because of fears or worries? Stop and take a moment to think about this.

The truth is, many of us have been there at some point where we get overwhelmed by fear, anxiety, or worries. Too afraid to speak or make a move.

Wouldn't you love to live a life where you feel confident and courageous? How about a life where you also feel connected, happy, and fulfilled because you are purposely pursuing your passion and you're on track with your goals and dreams?

I'm assuming that since you've picked up this book you are open to believing in the possibilities of what the future might hold and you desire to make changes that might be necessary to take your life from where you are at this moment to the level you wish.

I believe that, no matter what stage we're at in life, there is always room for improvement or always something to accomplish. I think deep down—whether consciously or subconsciously—every one of us wants to achieve our highest potential.

A popular quote by Oprah Winfrey says: *"Create the highest, grandest vision possible for your life, because you become what you believe."*

Now, this is where I should stop and tell you that I do not profess to be a guru or an expert in psychology. However, I have learned a lot throughout the years, and based on my personal experience, I've acquired valuable knowledge and insights that I plan to share with you in this book. My hope is that, no matter what might have happened in the past or no matter what you may encounter in the future, you never stop dreaming, never stop believing, never stop trusting, and never stop moving forward in a positive direction.

In addition to my personal experiences, I've also spent countless hours researching and understanding human emotions, changes, habits, behaviors, and success.

So, now, if you're ready to unleash your full potential, I'd like to invite you to come on this journey with me. My goal is to ignite a fire from deep within you so that you can step forward and start BELIEVING in the possibilities of your dreams. *I want you to always remember that if you think you can, YOU can.*

Indeed, what you believe could become your reality!

CHAPTER 1

GETTING UNSTUCK

Be willing to step outside your comfort zone once in a while; take the risks in life that seem worth taking. The ride might not be as predictable if you'd just planted your feet and stayed put, but it will be a heck of a lot more interesting.

- EDWARD WHITACRE, JR. -

* * *

So, that afternoon as I continued to look out of my window, I found myself wondering what would have happened if Les hadn't left his comfort zone to pursue his dreams of becoming a motivational speaker. Where would he be right now? There is no doubt that his life would be drastically different from what it is now. Les's decision to leap has taken him to places he had never gone before—to do things he had never done before— and to see people he had never seen before. In doing so, he has become highly successful at living his dreams—doing something he is passionate about.

I also wondered what would have happened if Tony hadn't decided one day that he'd had enough of the life he was living, working as a janitor and living in a dingy apartment.

Could you imagine that Tony was a janitor? The first time I read this, I thought I was seeing double, so of course I re-read it to confirm. Yes, sometimes I wonder a lot. If I was on Facebook or Twitter, this is where I would put the confused, questioning emoji (you might be familiar with the one with its hand by its face).

In any case, Tony knew deep down that he was capable of doing better, so he decided to quit his job, which was clearly beneath his intellectual capabilities. What would Tony's life look like if he hadn't aimed higher?

Through sweat and tears, Tony managed to work his way up from rock bottom and has positioned himself to become an extraordinary leader. Through his work, he has inspired and empowered many people from all walks of life: CEOs, entrepreneurs, politicians, professional athletes, musicians, authors, and doctors.

Many of us won't step outside of our comfort zones because we lack the courage and confidence to step up and out into our destinies.

We doubt whether *we **can do** what we say we're going to do*.

We doubt whether *we are **good enough, talented enough, or smart enough** to do what we say we're going to do.*

We worry about ***how** we're going to do what we plan to do* or whether we have all the resources (time, money, people, et cetera) we need in place to do what we want to do, and we worry about ***what others might think*** about us and what we want to say or do.

We doubt ourselves and worry so much that we remain stuck in the "can I?" mentality. Wouldn't it be great if we could move from the *"Can I?"* to the *"Yes, I can!"* way of thinking?

Wouldn't it be nice if we could just flip a switch, and presto, problem solved? No more holding back! No more wondering if we are good enough, pretty enough, intelligent enough, or talented enough.

No more wondering if we have what it takes to pursue a modeling career or if we are talented enough to pursue our dreams of becoming a successful actor, artist, or singer.

No more wondering if we are smart enough to get the job we want and deserve.

No more wondering if the business idea we have is good enough for us to run with or whether the books we're writing or the paintings we're painting or the product we've been developing are good enough.

No more wondering if we're eloquent enough to stand up and speak in front of a room full of people, and instead, we take the leap like Les Brown did and go for it.

I believe that no matter what we may be going through it is vital that we take comfort in knowing we are not alone—that many others have been in a similar situation and have managed to work their way through. It may also be reassuring to know that each of us is a unique, powerful, and talented individual who was put on this earth to make a difference.

Yes, we are incredible beings. Even if we were rejected by a parent, a grandparent, a sibling, a friend, a boss, a coworker, or an opportunity in the past, it doesn't mean that we should curl up, wither away, and die. This is the time to gather everything we have inside of us—to get up, ignite a fire, and steadfastly pursue whatever it is that we have our eyes and hearts set on. This is also the time when we can take comfort in knowing that sometimes we may not be able to move by our own strengths but we can be moved by the strength of our higher power (in my case, it's God, the Father, the Spirit, the Truth, the Light, or the Universe).

To develop the confidence and the courage to go after what we want usually involves a process. For many people, this process begins the minute they decide they no longer want to live a mediocre life—that they want more of whatever "more" is. In that moment, more might be more money, more time, more freedom, better health, better jobs, or healthier relationships, and this list could go on.

*

So the big question for you is: ***are you living the life you had envisioned for yourself—are you on track with your dreams and goals?***

Perhaps there is one thing at the top of your goals list. Maybe you aspire to become a successful entrepreneur, professional athlete, artist, author, musician, or something else. Or perhaps you're on track with your career and everything is going along well enough, but you're not passionate about what you're doing, and so you're looking forward to trying something new. Perhaps you have a desire to become healthier or to travel to places that you've never been before. Maybe you want to establish more fulfilling and healthier relationships, or perhaps you just want to have more time or more freedom. Whatever the case may be, my intent is to inspire and empower you to keep striving for the things you want to achieve.

You should never settle for less than you deserve, nor should you ever settle for less than you're capable of accomplishing.

If you are looking to make changes in your life and want to join me on this journey, here is what you should know:

- This book was written from the perspective of someone who has worn many shoes (executive, entrepreneur, wife, and mother, among other roles). Inside, I've shared valuable insights, tools, tips, strategies, exercises, and action plans to help you to create a shift so that you can focus on your daily activities, intentions, behaviors, and habits while you navigate your way to success in your career, business, finances, relationships, health, and any other areas you may wish to improve.

- I've also shared some of my personal life experiences, as well as the stories of super successful and extraordinary people (some of them you may recognize) to inspire you to let go of past events so you can learn to walk or stand on your story instead of dwelling in it. I want you to know that you too can overcome the pain of disappointments, setbacks, losses, and betrayals so you can focus on designing the life you want, one step at a time. Keep BELIEVING that you can create the grandest vision possible for your life.

- While this book can be read as a standalone, it is meant to be a follow-up to my previous book, *It's All Up to YOU.*

Inside the pages of this book, you'll also:

- Learn how I moved forward from the "Can I?" to the "Yes. I can" way of thinking.

- Learn how to maintain momentum and set winning goals and objectives using the powerful blueprint I developed and used to mentally prepare myself to focus on my *one thing*. You'll also learn how to use this blueprint to get organized in your work and home life.

- Learn about the subtle difference between our daily intentions and our goals. Yes, there is a difference!

- Learn how paying close attention to your daily habits, routines, attitudes, actions, and behaviors can define your future.

- Get inspired by real-life examples of super successful and extraordinary people who followed their heart, took a leap of faith, and managed to rise from the bottom to the top of their games.

- Learn how to develop actionable plans and set goals that are specific, measurable, attainable, realistic, and timely.

By the end of this book, you should also understand the following:

1. It is critical that we FOCUS on doing the things we know deep down we ought to be doing, especially as it pertains to fulfilling our life's purpose.

2. It is important to BELIEVE and OWN our dreams, and we should never stop pursuing them. We may get knocked down from time to time, and things might become difficult, but it is critical that, no matter what, we get back up and try again. When we hit rock bottom, we can either stay there or make a strong decision to rise up.

3. It is important that we maintain a positive ATTITUDE as we work on our goals and objectives. This is especially important during difficult times.

4. It's better to hang with POSITIVE people versus negative and toxic ones.

5. Small steps are just as important as big steps. Small WINS are also powerful!

6. There is something at play that is much BIGGER than you and I. Throughout this book, I refer to this Being as God or the Universe.

CHAPTER 2

YOU ARE THE MASTER OF YOUR DESTINY

You control your future, your destiny. What you think about comes about.

- MARK VICTOR HANSEN -

* * *

Have you ever stopped frozen in your tracks or sat up suddenly with eyes wide open with the full realization that you are the master of your *own* destiny—that you are indeed responsible for your *own* thoughts, attitudes, beliefs, actions, and behaviors? In many cases, being aware that we are indeed the master of our own destiny can profoundly impact our lives.

In life, we can choose the attitudes, habits, actions, and behaviors that will steer us in a positive direction, or we can choose the ones that will take us down a destructive path. We usually know when we are heading in the right direction because when we are on the right path, things usually seem to fall into place; for example, our health, relationships, finances, spirituality, and other areas will improve or flourish. We tend to feel more happy, peaceful, connected, confident, and hopeful.

On the other hand, when we are off track, things are usually the opposite. We tend to feel unhappy, restless, overwhelmed, doubtful, and fearful. Sometimes things can get out of balance so quickly that we may find ourselves standing in awe wondering what is happening in our lives. At times like these, we may even feel like throwing in the towels or throw a temper tantrum right in the middle of town. However, as much as we may feel like giving up, we cannot do that. At some point, and hopefully sooner than later, we must get our lives back on the right track. If we want to achieve the things we desire, it's essential that we get up, pull up our skirts (hopefully a fabulous one) or pants, and prepare to move forward confidently, courageously, and gracefully.

There is no doubt that it can be difficult, sometimes, to get through tough situations. However, with hope, faith, strength, courage, and determination, anything is possible. We can overcome our challenges and move on to live happy, productive, and fulfilled lives after a change.

*

TRUSTING THE PROCESS

Perhaps you're currently at a point in your life where you're having difficulties believing you can get to where you want to go. What I've learned is that if you trust the process, no matter what, eventually you will get there. **Never forget that you are the master of your own destiny—that your life belongs to you and only you.** Yes, there will be times when we might have to put the needs of others ahead of our own needs and desires. But at the end of the day, we must live our own lives. We must never be afraid to stare down our own truths and acknowledge the ones we care to own. It doesn't matter what may have happened in the past, because let's face it, we are all imperfect human beings and "life happens."

Sometimes things will cause us to get out of our games, but at some point, we must get back on track and continue to pursue the things we want to achieve the most in life. **It is critical that we make the choices and decisions that are right for us, no matter what.**

*

I've always known that I'm the master of my own destiny, and I was on the right track until, as I indicated before, "life happens." So, to get back on track, I decided I'd make 2017 the "Year of Me."

I wrote and published my first book *Honor Your Gifts in 2007*, and I didn't release another one until ten years later. Now, the fact that I wrote and published two books isn't something to brag about. No. I can't dance or wave my hand in the air either because it took me ten long, excruciating years before I wrote my second book *It's All Up to YOU*.

I've described this time as agonizing because I discovered that I was passionate about writing back in 2006. With this revelation, I planned and wanted to keep writing but still wasn't writing in any meaningful way because I was either too fearful, too doubtful, too worried, or too busy trying to balance my work and family life.

On the days when I wasn't too busy, I was too tired even to think straight. So, as much as I tried, I just couldn't get inspired. Even though I enjoyed writing, I just couldn't. I'd start writing, and then I'd stop. Rewrite. Start and stop. Rewrite. Start and stop. I kept kicking myself because I knew how to set and smash goals. After all, I've smashed a lot of goals before.

Every time I'd think about writing, I'd feel something stirring deep inside me. It was my gut trying to send me a strong signal that I should pay attention. It is an unpleasant feeling when you know deep down that you should be doing something, but you don't.

And so, there I was wondering what was wrong with me. It was then that I made a **conscious decision** to START from where I was, using what I have, the best way I could. It was as simple as that. I needed to make changes in my life, but first, I had to get out of my *own* head, and so I listened and began to write. It didn't matter whether it was morning, noon, or night, I'd seize the opportunity to write. I told myself enough was enough—no more nonsense!

I picked up some momentum when I told myself I'd spend a minimum of ten minutes each day to write. Eventually, I increased the time with little or no effort, and I didn't stop writing until I completed and published my last book mentioned above, in mid-2017. I plan to share more about this journey later in this book.

*

THINGS TO DO, PLACES TO GO, AND PEOPLE TO SEE

It is true; some of easiest things we could ever do may often seem to be the most painful. For example:

- We know we should start looking for a job or run with the business idea that we've been thinking about for some time now.

- We know we should call our bank or financial advisor to make arrangements to start stashing some funds away for a rainy day.

- We know we should start the book that we've been thinking about writing, or, better yet, that we should finish the one we've been rewriting for the umpteenth time.

- We know we should fit some exercise into our daily schedules.

- We know we should pick up the phone and call or visit a loved one.

If we should take a moment to stop and think, in many cases, we'll find the things we need to do are relatively straightforward, yet somehow, they seem far more difficult than they actually are.

It makes sense to me when James E. Faust said: *"Some of our important choices have a time line. If we delay a decision, the opportunity is gone forever. Sometimes our doubts keep us from making a choice that involves change. Thus an opportunity may be missed."*

Now, while, it is normal for us to have moments when we hesitate to act or speak up, if we want to create the ideal life we want, it is critical that we let go of whatever it is that is holding us back and make a conscious decision to move forward in a positive direction, no matter what.

Don't worry about the *hows*. Sometimes we spend far too much time worrying about how we're going to finish a project, or how we will afford to get things done, or how we're going to get to where we want to go, for example. You'll find that once you start to do what you set out to do, the *hows* will fall into place.

If you're thinking about painting a picture, you don't have to complete it in a day or even one week; focus on the vision of what you want your art to look like and make preparations to do just a few strokes at a time.

Likewise, if you plan to write a book, the chances are you already know what you want to write about. It's just a matter of getting your thoughts out of your head and putting them down on paper. So, why not consider spending ten minutes or so each day to focus on writing? You can even begin by writing just a few paragraphs. You may be surprised to see how much momentum you may pick up, and before you know it, you'll be well on your way to publishing that book. Don't worry about perfecting your words or your grammar. You'll have lots of time to go back and expand or correct your thoughts later.

If you plan to look for a job, why not start updating your resume immediately? You can send a few copies of your newly updated résumé to the companies on your list within the next few days; if you have a résumé readily available, why not start sending some out today? If you're thinking Gosh, I sent out a gazillion of them already with no positive response; it doesn't matter; today might just be your day—just give it another try. Never give up on doing the things that could positively impact your life. If you never start, you'll never find out where your journey may take you. Think about it.

Even when things seem impossible, keep believing because usually what you think will become your reality. This is where having a strong vision and a strong faith will come in.

The key is *really* in starting. If you don't try, you won't make progress.

*

Everything shifted for me when I *decided* I wanted more of the best things that life has to offer: prosperity, progress, good health, love, happiness, peace, and success. I started to BELIEVE that I was capable of accomplishing what I'd set out to do. That I'd let go of my fears, doubts, worries, and hang-ups, and grasp onto the knowledge that I am indeed a remarkable, powerful, unique, talented, blessed, yet imperfect human being. (Hey, don't get me wrong. I'm still a work in progress. I've got a lot of people to see, a lot of places to go, and a whole lot of things to do. I'm still moving).

I've since named the program I designed by fluke the *Start with 10 Success Blueprint (S10 Success Blueprint or S10S Blueprint)*, and Start with 10 means just that—start with 10. I plan to share more details about this blueprint with you later in this book. It's a BONUS.

Today, writing has become a significant part of my life. It has changed my life on so many different levels, and it all started with that one **conscious decision**—to spend a minimum of ten minutes each day to focus on doing the *one thing* I knew deep down I ought to be doing. From there, I started to make other positive changes in my life.

*

My momentum began the moment I stopped holding back and stopped striving for perfection. What I've come to realize is when we strive for perfect it will steal our time, energy, and resources because when we are busy trying to perfect something or keep thinking we ought to get something just right, we tend to get tired and overwhelmed, and we may never start or continue to do the things we intended to do.

The plan and strategies I'd put in place with the *Start with 10 Success Blueprint* helped me to stay on track with the vision I have for my writing. This blueprint has allowed me to become more organized and effective at work and at home. For example, I use it to help me with my morning routines. As a busy mom, this is a huge win for me because it means the kids will be off to school on time, and I'd get to focus on my goals for the day a lot sooner.

Have you had moments when you wish you'd just had a few more minutes? I think many of us have been there.

Just a few more minutes and you wouldn't have had to drive the kids all the way to school because as you pulled around the corner, the bus moved off. And, the light! If you hadn't hit that red light, you might have managed to catch up to the bus at the next stop. Now, this tardiness added an extra twenty minutes to your morning—time that you *really* don't have.

Just a few more minutes and you wouldn't be late for your doctor's appointment, and now you have to sit around for another twenty or thirty minutes because the patient that was after you was early and took your spot.

Just a few more minutes and you would have gotten to your crucial business meeting on time, and now your boss is giving you *that* look that's making you wish you could shrink.

Just a few more minutes and you would have gotten to church before the choir started to sing your favorite song—you only caught the tail end. How annoying?

Now, you get the point. During times like those mentioned above, the *S10S Blueprint* might prove to be valuable.

CHAPTER 3

IF YOU THINK YOU, CAN YOU CAN

People spend too much time finding other people to blame, too much energy finding excuses for not being what they are capable of being, and not enough energy putting themselves on the line, growing out of the past, and getting on with their lives.

- J. MICHAEL STRACZYNSKI -

* * *

As I've said before, we all have dreams or at least things we want to accomplish. It doesn't matter how big or how small our dreams are; what's important is that we stay true to them. Some of us tend to lose sight of the things we desire because we may run into challenges, and sometimes, instead of trying to figure things out as we go along, we throw in the towels. I honestly think some of us give up on our dreams far too soon. If people who have experienced tougher challenges can push past their fears, doubts, and worries to achieve things which are indescribable, then, so can you and I. Stop for a moment and think about it. There is hope!

There is a popular quote by Henry Ford that says: *"Whether you think you can, or think you can't, you're right."* This means the power lies in our thinking and our attitude toward accomplishing something. For example, if we believe we can do something, then we will find a way to get it done, even if the climb gets incredibly steep. On the other hand, if we think we cannot accomplish something, then more than likely we will not give it everything we've got. We might give up somewhere along the way, and as I've said before, usually what we believe will become reality.

Lately, I've been saying: *If you think you can, YOU can. If you can't, then, fake it until you can.*

Sometimes when some people hear the word "fake" they tend to get into a tizzy, but the truth is, many people have faked it until they made it.

That's right!

Many people (some of them you may know) have started things that they weren't sure about, but then they figured "it" out along the way and achieved tremendous success. Entrepreneurs are great examples of people who have had to fake it. Many of them started businesses and didn't have a clue about how to run a business—all they had was an idea, but through trial and error, they were able to move on to become highly successful. Today some of them are our world's best leaders.

In the opening pages of this book, I used Les Brown as an example of someone who at first hesitated to trust his vision. He eventually moved forward and has become successful.

Joel Osteen is another person who had experienced doubts and fears. He said he wasn't sure if he could lead a congregation when he had to step into his father's shoes many years ago. However, he did and has become a huge success, making positive differences in the lives of many people around the world.

Barbara Corcoran, who is best known for her role as one of the dragons on *Shark Tank*, didn't know she would become super successful in real estate; she had doubts and worries, especially when she encountered difficult challenges along the way. However, Barbara was motivated to keep going because she knew she was capable of achieving more. Albeit, it might have helped that she didn't want her ex to have the satisfaction of seeing her fail. I guess there's truth to these sayings *Sometimes you just gotta do what you gotta do"* or *"who laughs last laughs best."*

What Barbara also didn't know is that she would write a bestselling book, *Shark Tales: How I Turned $1,000 into a Billion Dollar Business*. This $1,000, by the way, was borrowed from her ex to start her real estate business.

It is so easy for many of us to not think about the things we want to do or achieve. We often tell ourselves we'll get them done someday. Really? Someday?

What many of us should realize is that procrastination isn't going to get us what we want. Procrastination won't get us the houses or cars we desire. Procrastination won't take us on *that* much-needed vacation. It won't send our kids to college or university or help us to save for our retirement. Procrastination won't build relationships. It won't pick up the phone to connect with our loved ones, and it definitely can't say "I'm thinking about you" or "I love you."

If you are at the stage where you know you should be making changes, whether financially, emotionally, physically, or spiritually, then make your someday today or tomorrow, not next week, not next month, or next year.

Here are some critical questions for you to answer as honestly as you can:

- When it comes to your dreams, are you willing to do what it takes to achieve the ones you desire the most?

- Are you consciously and steadfastly working to achieve the things which are important to you? If your answer is yes, then that's great. However, if your answer is no, then, my next question to you will be: Why not? What are you going to do about it?

- Do you have a goals list? If you don't have a goals list, I'd suggest that you start one immediately. Did you know that most successful people have written goals and they work hard at developing steps and implementing strategies to help them achieve them?

*

FEAR IS A NORMAL HUMAN REACTION

Fear is described as an unpleasant feeling of apprehension or distress caused by the presence or anticipation of danger. Many of us have experienced this emotion at one time or another. It is a normal human reaction which can often make us feel paralyzed and helpless.[1] As such, we tend to avoid people and situations

---

[1] An article on anxiety can be read at: http://www.mayoclinic.org/diseases-conditions/generalized-anxiety-disorder/basics/definition/con-20024562

that make us feel fearful. Harriet Lerner, the author of *Fear and Other Uninvited Guests* says:

> Fear is not something to be conquered or eliminated—or even tackled, for that matter. Instead, we may need to pay close attention to its message. Most of us experience fear as a kind of stop sign or flashing red light that warns: "Danger! Do not enter!" But we may need to decode that signal and consider what it's trying to convey. What is the actual nature of the danger? Is it past or present, real or imagined? Are we feeling anxious because we are boldly charting new territory, or because we're about to do something stupid?[2]

It is important to understand the difference between outright fear and anxiety, which is a type of fear marked by worrying. Although anxiety is usually not as drastic as fear, it can still have a grave effect on us—it's as though we're being fearful at a lower intensity but often on a more constant basis.

Experts say when fear confronts us, we should stop to ask ourselves if our fear is reasonable. Is it real or imagined?

I believe we were created to be powerful, fearless, and courageous. However, somewhere along the way, we were taught to become more cautious. When there seemed to have been some perceived danger, we were forced to take a step back or abort our mission altogether.

The following verse in 2 Timothy, Chapter 1:7 reminds us about the authentic power that God gave us upon creation:

---

[2] *Fear and Other Uninvited Guests*, Harriet Lerner, 2004

For God hath not given us the spirit of fear, but of power, and of love, and of sound mind.

*

COPING WITH FEAR

The following can assist you in dealing with (or forgetting) about your fears:

- Set goals and focus on affirmations to help you to overcome your fears.

  Affirmations usually begin with an "I am," "I can," or "I will" statement. For example, I am courageous, I am emotionally healthy, or I will survive this difficult time.

- If your fear isn't real (meaning there is no valid reason to be fearful), keep reassuring yourself that it isn't.

- Talk about your fears with the people you trust.

- Understand you cannot control everything, but you can control how you react to certain things. Step back and relax when you feel the need to take control.

- Meditate and participate in activities that will help you to relax and breathe appropriately. Keep reflecting on positive thoughts. Try to meditate on a daily basis. Practice deep breathing (in through your nose) and exhaling (out through your mouth) for approximately five to ten minutes each time. Depending on the severity of your problem, you might want to do this a few times each day. There are many good books and other resources available online that can offer you some good meditative strategies.

- Try handing over your fears to God (also known as the Universe, the Spirit, the Truth, the Light, the Source). Keep praying about it. Ask God to give you the strength and courage to help you to face your fears head-on. Remember that nothing is too big for him to handle.

- Read motivational books, including the *Bible*. The Book of Psalms offers encouragement for dealing with negative emotions. If you don't own a *Bible*, get an app. There are many resources available online, including some free e-Book versions that can be downloaded from various online retailers.

Understand that you cannot control everything, but you can control how you react to certain things. Step back and relax when you feel the need to take control.

*

BE WILLING TO DO WHAT IT TAKES

If you are ready to go steadfast in the pursuit of your dreams, know that it will take a lot of time, patience, courage, and determination to make things happen. If you are serious about building your dreams, it might take a lot of sleepless nights and long, long days, because hard work is never easy or sexy, for that matter. Be prepared to get downright messy and dirty as you hustle and grind your way through any obstacles you may face.

. . . .

If you are ready to go after your dreams, know that it will take a lot of time, patience, courage, and determination to make things happen.

. . . .

*

PERSONAL MISSION STATEMENTS

Did you know Walt Disney's mission was to make people happy? His goal was to bring smiles to children's faces. Mother Teresa's purpose was to love and accept others, and she did this with passion and conviction.

Writing out your mission statement can ensure you have clarity and you never lose sight of your **intentions** as you continue to pursue your endeavors. In other words, your personal mission statement will help you to stay focused on important matters.

Your personal mission statement will evolve over time, as you continue to grow and as other things become more important to you.

Years ago, when I went on a quest to find truer meaning, I realized I had not been living in God's grace, and I certainly was not fulfilling the purpose he had intended for my life.

It was also important to me that no matter what may occur in my life that I remain a good mother. I have been blessed with two beautiful children, and it is my ultimate responsibility to love and teach them to be the best they can be. With all this in mind, I decided to write my personal mission statement. I felt I needed something to remind me of what was *really* important in my life.

The following is an excerpt of my personal mission statement as written in my book, *Honor Your Gifts* (2007):

> While I was continuing my search, I realized that over the previous several years I had not been living in God's grace, and I certainly was not fulfilling the purpose he had intended for me. Developing this book has helped me to realize that I've always had a passion for writing, especially about more meaningful things—the type of things that really matter in life. I wanted my words to reach people in a profound way.

It was also very important to me that I was a good mother. God has blessed me with two wonderful children: he gave them to me for a purpose, and it is my ultimate responsibility to teach them to be the best that they can be and to grow up to be good, loving, and responsible adults.

With all this in mind, I decided to write my own personal mission statement. I felt I needed something to remind me of what was really important in fulfilling my purpose.

Today, my personal mission statement looks something like this:

"To use my writing to inspire and empower others to keep pursuing their dreams, no matter what obstacles they may face along their life's journey, and to teach my kids to become kind, loving, productive, and responsible adults. I will strive to live my life with passion, honesty, and integrity."

TIP: If you haven't had a chance to complete a **personal mission statement** yet, now would be a great time to do one. It doesn't have to be perfect; just write something that's meaningful.

Think about the things and people who are important to you in both your work and home life, and work around those. Perhaps, you already know what your life's missions are, but writing them out can ensure you never lose sight of your intentions as you go about your daily business.

CHAPTER 4

DEVELOPING A SUCCESSFUL MINDSET

Your mindset matters. It affects everything—from the business and investment decisions you make, to the way you raise your children, to your stress levels and overall well-being.

- PETER DIAMANDIS -

* * *

There is no doubt our mindsets, attitudes, habits, actions, and behaviors matter—among other things, they can determine how far we can go to accomplish positive things in our lives.

In *It's All Up to YOU*, I wrote about the difference in mindsets between four groups of people: The Fortunate Ones (also referred to as the Smart Ones), the Modest Ones, the Frivolous Ones, and the Lazy Ones (also referred to as the Unfortunate Ones). I've provided a brief description of the various groups below:

- **The Fortunate Ones** (if they did not receive a huge inheritance or win the lottery) are usually high achievers. Some of these people could also be referred to as the

"Smart Ones" because more than likely they became successful by working hard and developing healthy habits, attitudes, and behaviors to get to where they are presently at. The Fortunate Ones are persistent and strive to make the right choices and decisions as they move along in life. Some of the people in this group have a big bank account and can afford to purchase big homes, expensive clothes, jewelry, and cars if they choose to.

- **The Modest Ones** desire a more modest lifestyle. They may work hard, but they will often put family above fame and fortune. The people in this group usually have modest homes and drive modest cars. Sometimes the people in this group could achieve more material things, or as we'd sometimes say, they can "live a little," but they're satisfied with what they have. Instead of indulging in frivolous things or activities, many of them prefer to give to others or donate to charities and societies.

- **The Frivolous Ones** are the people who are usually in need of a major "mind makeover." The Frivolous Ones are typically people in their thirties, forties, fifties, and sixties who still haven't figured out how to manage their time, life, or money. They have enormous responsibilities, but they are still living in a bubble. I call these people "frivolous" because they know they're not doing what should be done, yet the Frivolous Ones keep making the same mistakes day after day and then beat themselves up each time, not realizing that if they want a different result, they have to do things differently. Some of the people in this group are smart, kind, and hardworking individuals, but they spend their money as if there is no tomorrow. They live like the Fortunate Ones, except there is no big bank account. The Frivolous Ones tend to live from paycheck to paycheck, and to top things off, some of them are not thinking about the inevitable.

- **The Lazy Ones** lack the motivation to get up and try to make something of their lives; they have no vision for their future and will more than likely blame others for their failures. The people in this group are usually in need of a major "mind reconstruction." Some of the people in this group might have significant issues: low self-esteem, mental illnesses, emotional issues, and/or alcohol or drug addictions. If it turns out that there is more to the story, then perhaps these people can be called the Unfortunate Ones and we can give them a bit of a break.

*

Karen Salmansohn says: "When you have a 'solution thinking mindset'—and choose to focus 80% of your thoughts/words on solutions—you will not only be heading more speedily to long-term success, but you will immediately feel better in the moment."

Actor and comedian Kevin Hart says: *"No matter what, people grow. If you chose not to grow, you're staying in a small box with a small mindset. People who win go outside of that box. It's very simple when you look at it."*

What's fascinating about Kevin Hart is that he persisted in following his dreams even when others doubted his capabilities. Kevin says that a powerful and well-known individual in the entertainment industry told him years ago that he should find something else to do because he didn't think comedy was "it" for him. Can you believe that?

Kevin said he couldn't believe that he was told he was no good to his face. He said: *"Nobody knows your future but you. Nobody can predict your outcome but you."*

Kevin's story is an excellent example of why we shouldn't pay too much attention to our doubters and our naysayers.

If someone doubts, criticizes, or tell us outright that we shouldn't pursue something, we should learn to ignore them and persist, especially when we feel that we're heading in the right direction.

*

YOUR NEXT STEPS

What do you have to do to make your dream a reality? Can you determine what it is you want the most of? For example: Do you have your eyes set on a new position at your workplace? If this is the case, perhaps you might want to improve your qualifications. Do you need to talk to someone about it? Do you need to take additional courses to bring yourself up to speed? Perhaps you could find a mentor who would be willing to teach you things that would be relevant to that position? Take a good look around you; is there anyone in your current circle who could teach you something new (a grandparent, parent, sibling, friend, or colleague)? If you cannot find anyone in your circle, then step outside of it. Get to know other people. Start networking. In many cases, we'll find that we may need to venture outside our circles or comfort zones to get the things we want. You might want to offer to assist whoever is willing to support you for free; then they can, in turn, teach you all they can.

Do you have a desire to start your own business? Perhaps, your next steps would be to start saving enough money to start that venture. You could also start learning all that you can about the industry you'd like to tap into. Do you need to take some business courses or find other ways to learn more about that particular industry or other relevant information that might relate to your new idea?

How about a plan to start saving for your kids' education or your retirement?

How about saving for a down payment on a home? If you are planning to purchase a home, have you given any thought to the type of house you want? How much will you need for the down payment?"

Do you plan to start your own family? If so, you might want to start saving. It's more than likely that you will need to take some time off to care for your child. You'll certainly need to prepare for the birth of your child.

Perhaps your dream is to pursue that *one thing* that sets your heart on fire. You are already talented and have all the know-hows; if this is the case, then what doors do you need to knock on?

No matter what you want to pursue, consciously think about your next steps and endeavor to keep moving forward, no matter what.

*

KEEP PURSUING YOUR PASSION AND DREAMS

If you have a dream, never stop pursuing it. If you are already on your journey, never stop doing what it is that is feeding your soul or is getting you what you desire. When I think of people who steadfastly continued to do what they love, I think of people like Betty White (who just celebrated her ninety-sixth birthday and is still going strong), Maya Angelou, Nelson Mandela, and Mother Teresa. Though these people might have slowed down a bit in their ripe old age, they never stopped doing what they loved and didn't hold back to do all they could to make a difference in the lives of others.

I've heard this said before: Do something you love, and it won't seem like work.

*

MY EIGHT-STEP STRATEGY FOR DEVELOPING A POWERFUL MINDSET

So, if you are dissatisfied with where you're at in life, are you prepared to step outside of your box (otherwise known as your comfort zone)? Are you willing to make the necessary changes to create a life that will allow you to achieve your fullest potential? If your answer is yes, I've determined eight steps to help you to develop a powerful mindset. This process helped me tremendously to zero in on what I needed to focus on and where I needed to spend my time and efforts.

- **The first step** is to determine WHAT it is that you want the most of and then make a strong determination to pursue it. You must be more than willing to do what it takes to achieve your goal—you'll need to determine that you want more of what it is you believe is lacking in your life, whether you desire to have more money, more time, or more freedom, better health, a better job, or healthier relationships, et cetera.

  Get crystal clear on what it is you want more of, and then take a leap of faith.

- **The second step** is to decide WHY you want what you want. You cannot wholeheartedly pursue something if you're not sure why you're pursuing it. Once you understand your WHY, make it compelling, and then use it to illuminate your path going forward. Avoid distractions—stay focused on the people and things that motivate you the most.

  See Chapter 7 on how to develop a stronger WHY.

- **The third step** is to BELIEVE that you are capable of achieving whatever it is you want. Experts, teachers, and philosophers believe when you set a goal you should dream it and believe it. Some recommend you try to feel yourself living that vision. Try to think about your vision just before you go to bed at night, and think about it again the minute you are awake in the mornings. Your energy will help to make your dream a reality. This is where having a strong vision and a strong faith will come in. With a strong faith, you'll become confident in knowing you are not just relying on your strength and power, but you are also relying on the strength of your higher power to see you through. I find the following quote reassuring:

I can do all things through Christ who strengthens me.

- Philippians 4:13 -

See Chapter 11 for further details on how to develop a stronger vision.

- **The fourth step** is to decide on the ACTION steps (activities) that will help you to achieve your goals. You can wish, visualize, and be positive all you want, but if you do not ACT, nothing is going to happen. The sad thing is, many of us have a lot of great ideas, but if we don't follow through or even know which steps to take next, we're not going to achieve our goals. Therefore, it is imperative that we lay out each level, starting from

Step #1. Sometimes, we may need to make changes to our plan, but we can do so as we proceed. The big thing is to START. As you begin to move, things will become a lot clearer. So start where you're at, using what you have.

Focus on the steps you'll need to take you from where you are now to where you want to go.

- **The fifth** step is to decide WHEN you're going to do what you say you're going to do. Will this activity or goal take place in a month, six months, a year, or in five years? Again, we can have great ideas, but if we never start, things may never get done in a timely manner. Set a date to start, and then establish an end date.

Get it done so that you can enjoy your accomplishments and move on to the next "big" thing. *That's right! When you've achieved a goal, move on to the next one on your list.*

Also see Chapter 13 for further details on how to set and achieve S.M.A.R.T. goals.

- **The sixth step** is to APPLY—work hard at achieving what it is that you want.

It is critical that you remain focused, consistent, and persistent. If you must, find ways to go under, over, and through any obstacles that may stand between you and your goals. Never give up until you have found a solution to any problem you may encounter, because as sure as your butt points to the ground, you will encounter problems. **Of course, you have to be smart about the way you go about getting things done. Also, there is a fine line between learning when to walk away from something and when to continue working at it. If your gut is telling you that you're on the right track, then keep moving in *that* direction**.

- **The seventh step** is to ANALYZE your results. Figure out what works for you and what didn't. Look at your methods, patterns, action steps, habits, behaviors, attitudes, feelings, et cetera.

  Continue to do more of whatever it is that's moving you closer to your goals and dreams.

- **The eighth step** is to REPEAT, REPEAT, and REPEAT.

I cannot express how important it is to keep repeating whatever it is you're doing, especially if you're seeing some progress. Remember that success doesn't happen overnight. For example, if your goal is to become a successful author, you cannot simply write a book and when it didn't become an instant bestseller think that it's not going to work and give up on your dream. No, you don't. Believe that you are making a difference. And as Tyler Perry advised: "keep planting your seeds, keep watering them, and keep believing."

So, in this case, move on to writing the next book, and the next, and the next. Trust that your audience will find you, eventually. They may come across one book and love it, and kaboom! They now have access to two or three more of your books, and then they begin to tell others about you and your work.

The same could apply to anything else. For example, if you believe a product or service you want to offer is better than the ones that are currently available, then you might want to pursue that goal of developing and marketing that product or service.

EXERCISE:

Now, it's time for some tough questions. I encourage you to take some time to think about your answers over the next few days:

a) What is the *one thing* that you want to do the most—the one you know deep down would change your life in a profound way?

____

____

b) Does this *one thing* scare you?   Yes ☐ No ☐

c) Do you think you **can** or **can't** do what you want to do?

Can ☐ Can't ☐

d) If the answer to c) above is can, are you on track with your goals/actions? If your answer is yes, great, keep moving. If your answer is no, why not? Get on with it. Remember that small steps are just as important as big steps. You may find the *S10S Blueprint* even more powerful.

e) If the answer to c) above is can't, then may I ask what is holding you back? Think about it, and then write down all the things you believe are preventing you from pursuing your *one thing*. Once you can make some determinations, I urge you to work hard at overcoming whatever it is you may need to overcome.

____

____

CHAPTER 5

KEEP DREAMING

Stay true to yourself, yet always be open to learn. Work hard, and never give up on your dreams, even when nobody else believes they can come true but you. These are not clichés but real tools you need no matter what you do in life to stay focused on your path.

- PHILLIP SWEET -

* * *

No matter who you are, where you're from or where you're going. Whether you're just starting out in life, or whether you've been trudging along for some time on this journey we call life; whether your dreams got delayed, derailed, or obliterated, keep on dreaming.

Stop being fearful—stop doubting—stop worrying—stop hesitating—stop procrastinating, and stop being sad.

Sometimes, it can be challenging to let go of any negative emotions that we may be feeling. If you are experiencing any undesirable emotions at this time, I suggest you learn coping strategies to help you to deal with them appropriately. It is essential that you do what is necessary to get well. My previous book *It's All Up to YOU* offers many insightful tools, tips, and strategies for feeling, doing, and living better. You can check it out if you think it would be beneficial to your health and well-being.

Remember: If you think you can, YOU can!

*

Now, imagine waking up one day with the realization that you'd be heading home to spend the Christmas holiday with loved ones. You're super excited for the food, the company, the music, the gifts, the hugs, the kisses, and everything else that comes along with the good stuff in life.

You can't stop thinking about your trip. You've been waiting for weeks. You packed, got dressed, packed some more (among other things, of course), and off you went. You boarded the plane, sat down, buckled your seat, leaned back, and exhaled. You'll be home soon (or so you thought) because how would you have known that something dreadful was about to happen—something that would change your life and the lives of your loved ones forever?

When you woke up, you realized you weren't where you thought you'd be, but instead you're in a hospital fighting to hold on to dear life. You have a faint memory of what had happened moments before it did. There are still many unanswered questions. The one thing you know for sure— things have changed drastically, and your hopes and dreams are dashed. Your future doesn't look anything like the one you had envisioned a year or even a month prior.

The story below is a reminder that changes are indeed inevitable.

Note: The event is real; however, the activities surrounding these events are made up, because, hello, I do know a thing or two about traveling.

Read on!

*

A BEAUTY THAT RADIATES FROM WITHIN

One night as I was watching America's Got Talent 2017, I heard Kechi Okwuchi would be performing. It was the first time I had heard of her. The producers gave a brief description about her journey, and so I was intrigued. Kechi walked onto the stage with amazing confidence. She stood courageously and poised, and then she faced the crowd and started to sing in a voice that transcended it all. Yes, this girl can sing!

Kechi has a beauty that radiates from within, and to me that is the essence of true beauty. Kechi's story is not an ordinary one (it's heart breaking), but yet there she stood, fearlessly, in front of a live audience with the awareness she would be seen by millions of people from all over the world. Looking at Kechi you could tell she had faced tremendous challenges but she wasn't letting anything stop her. She was confidently and courageously pursuing her dreams of becoming a singer.

Later, I learned Kechi was involved in a Sosoliso Airlines plane crash in 2005 that had left her clinging for her life.

There was a total of 109 passengers in this crash, and she was one of two people who survived. Kechi said while she was lying in bed for days, covered from head to toe with bandages, what kept her going was listening to music. She is an epitome of someone who has picked herself up and is moving forward, literally (By the way, I've seen pictures of Kechi prior to the plane crash, and she was a beautiful girl, and as far as I'm concerned, she still is. Kechi's beauty now radiates from within.).

Kechi believes she survived for a reason and wants to honor the victims of the crash by simply "living." Thankfully, she survived to provide hope and inspiration to others. Her story is a reminder to many of us that we should never stop pursuing our dreams. Unfortunately, Kechi only made it to the top ten on the show, but in my books, she is a winner. Her story is a true testament that no matter how difficult things may get, we can still use our disappointments, setbacks, and losses to make a difference in the lives of others. A story can lift the heart of another, and through faith, hope, and prayers, we shall overcome.

If Kechi can overcome obstacles and live her dreams, then it's possible for many of us, isn't it? Especially for many who have never had to deal with tremendous health issues.

Kechi thought she could, and guess what? She did.
You go, girl!

*

AN EXAMPLE OF A POSITIVE CHANGE

When compared to Kechi's story, Nathan's story might seem like an ordinary one, but it's a positive story nevertheless. This could be your story—just a simple one. Read on!

*

Nathan was in his late twenties when he realized his life wasn't heading in the right direction. He was bouncing around from one laboring job to the next. Many of Nathan's friends had graduated from university and were now working at well-paid jobs. Some were also married with young families.

Nathan's dating life was not much different from his work life, but the good news is that Nathan knew he was capable of achieving more, and so he decided to do something about his life. He quit his full-time job and went back to school to upgrade his education. Eventually, he enrolled in university and is now in his final year of studies. During this time, Nathan got married. He also found a job in his field of study with plans to work full-time while he finishes his degree on a part-time basis. Nathan is happy with the way his life has turned out. ***He believed he could and so he did***. Nathan stopped making excuses for his inactions and decided to make improvements to his life.

How about you? Do you find yourself making excuses for your inactions? If you are, what's holding you back?

*

YOUR ONE THING

I'd like you to take a moment to think about something that you've always wanted to do, but have lacked the courage and confidence to move forward with it. What is the first thing that comes to your mind? Grab onto whatever it is, and focus on that *thing* as we move along. Whatever it is, don't let go of it just yet.

*

DO NOT FALL BACK ON EXCUSES

To get things done, sometimes we'll need to spend our time more wisely, so for me to accomplish my goal of writing and publishing two books within a year, while working and taking care of my family, meant I had to say no to some people, invites, and unnecessary home-and-work-related tasks. I also had to say no to a lot of my kids' social activities. I told myself that it's a sacrifice all family members had to make.

As you move forward, think about what sacrifices you'd be willing to make. Whatever you do, do NOT fall back on excuses.

Remember: If you think you can, YOU can!

Keep dreaming, keep believing, but more importantly, keep moving, because as long as you're moving, you'll be bound to make progress.

Chapter 11 will provide you with more ideas for when you can say no to the people and things that won't move you forward.

*

WHAT YOU BELIEVE COULD BECOME YOUR REALITY

Some of us may wake up one day and decide that we no longer want to live a mediocre life and work hard at implementing changes. For some, a transformation begins the moment when their lives hit rock bottom, perhaps due to the loss of a job, income, business, a divorce, a severe illness, or other painful events. J.K. Rowling and Dwayne Johnson are a few examples of people whose lives had hit rock bottom. They were smart, courageous, and determined to keep moving despite getting knocked down on multiple occasions.

J.K. Rowling, for example, experienced the loss of her mother and a divorce before rising from poverty to create extreme wealth and affluence, thanks to her bestselling Harry Potter book series. Rowling credits much of her success to her painful past and personal losses and *owns* the fact that she built her incredible life from rock bottom. It has been reported that Rowling has a net worth of over one billion dollars and is now known to be one of the world's wealthiest women.

In Dwayne's case, he managed to pick himself up after his dream of becoming a professional football player in the United States' National Football League (NFL) was shattered due to a high school injury. Although he recovered, he realized that his injury wouldn't allow him to pursue a career in the NFL as planned. So, Dwayne decided that if he couldn't play for the NFL, he'd play for the Canadian Football League (CFL) and then he'd return to the NFL after he became a better player. In 1995 he got his big break and started playing for the CFL but got cut from the team within three months of arriving. Dwayne was devastated once again; however, he didn't give up. He kept putting one foot in front of the other. He finally decided that he'd get back into training, so he started going to the gym regularly. Dwayne was familiar with the wrestling world (his father and grandfather were both professional wrestlers, and his mother was a professional wrestling promoter), and eventually, Johnson was able to move on to become successful, first in the WWE and then as an actor. Johnson was the highest paid actor in 2016.

The above stories are proof once again that our mindsets, attitudes, habits, and behaviors have a lot to do with how far we can go to accomplish positive things in our lives.

These super successful people imagined a positive outcome, believed in their dreams, their capabilities, and the possibilities, trusted their guts and the Universe, and kept moving against any resistance they might have faced.

. . . .

**Some people succeed and some don't because
some have a strong vision for their lives
and work hard to achieve success.**

. . . .

*

If fears, doubts, and worries are preventing you from moving forward, know that you are not alone. As shown in the earlier stories, many of us have been there (myself included).

The chances are that since you've picked up this book, you're more than willing to do all the things which are necessary to take your life in a positive direction. Remember that you can move from where you are at any moment, no matter how insurmountable things might seem. Trust that eventually you will get to where you want to go. All you need is to make a firm decision just to start, and the rest will follow. Keep thinking clearly and effectively and then act on your choices.

In case you're thinking you don't have everything you need within you right at the moment, trust that you do and it will come out when you least expect it.

Keep calling it out. When that "thing" ignites within you, it will continue to burn bright if you keep fanning the flames.

Remember: If you think you can, YOU can!

*

STAY MOTIVATED

As you move forward, focus on the people and things that motivate you. Keep pushing yourself. Find a positive thought or mantra that reminds you to keep believing, whenever you need that nudge or push. Barbara Corcoran has said whenever she would think of giving up that she'd try to think or do something a different way just because she didn't want others to laugh at her. That thought worked for her.

My children illuminate my path. On days when I don't feel like moving, the thought of them helps me to get up and move. My husband and my parents also motivate me. I want to be a beacon of light for all of them.

CHAPTER 6

KEEP BELIEVING

Believe in yourself! Have faith in your abilities! Without a humble but reasonable confidence in your own powers you cannot be successful or happy.

- NORMAN VINCENT PEALE -

* * *

Have you ever wondered why some people seem to succeed at everything they do? No matter what they do, they seem to soar. They have great jobs, beautiful homes and nice cars, happy marriages, and healthy relationships. And on top of everything, they travel extensively and eat out at fancy restaurants regularly. To the onlookers, some may say "They have it all."

Do they have some success secrets or lessons to teach us? What can we learn from them? (Also see Chapter 12 for insights on learning and teaching.)

Here are some additional questions that we may want to find the answers to:

1. Is it because these people are blessed beyond measures?

2. Is it because they were in the right places at the right time (meaning lucky)?

3. Is it because these successful people have worked hard to achieve their goals, and have developed good habits—they have the right attitudes—and back each decision up with unrelenting action?

This is what I think. I'd say numbers one and two might contribute to a door opening. However, because a door opens, it doesn't mean that a person will succeed. It's what we do after the doors are open that can mean the difference between success and failure. Also, some people work hard but still cannot seem to accomplish anything significant.

I believe some people succeed and some don't because some have a strong vision for their lives and work hard to achieve their dreams. People with a success mindset also don't give up easily. They strive to get back up, no matter how many things life may throw their way—they view failures and setbacks as an opportunity to rise again, stronger and wiser.

Successful people believe in themselves and work to develop good habits, attitudes, and routines that complement or fit within their visions. They back up their ideas with actions and strive to remain focused and consistent with their endeavors. They persist even if the results they see are insignificant.

*

YOU ARE MORE THAN ENOUGH!

Now, is there something that you feel you should be doing, but you lack the confidence to move forward? Your gut might be telling you that this is the direction you should go in, but you're still not convinced. You keep asking yourself the "what if" questions:

What if I fail?

What if I can't?

What if this "thing" that I want to do turns out to be a complete disaster?

Along with the above questions, you might be feeling a sense of dread. Let me say this: Believe that you are ENOUGH! No matter what may be going on, find a way to start, and then take a tiny step forward. *In many cases, you'll find that it's better to take small steps, anyway, because in this case, your risks and stress level will be low also.*

And even if things don't turn out the way you'd hoped, you can take some comfort in knowing that you tried—you gave it your best shot. What lessons did you learn? What would you do differently? Did you grow? Did you acquire any skills and insights that you could transfer to something else?

Never underestimate what you can offer to the world. There might be someone waiting for just *your thing*—your product, your service, your song, your painting, your art, your book or poem, or anything else that you may have to offer.

Think about this long and hard. If you do, you'll realize that you're capable of changing lives. Keep believing in yourself and your abilities. Keep focusing on that *one thing* that you can feel from deep within you—that thing that keeps stirring your soul constantly—that thing that keeps you up at night—that thing that pops in your thoughts as you go about your daily business. What is it?

· ·

Never underestimate what you

can offer the world.

· ·

*

IGNORE THE LIES!

It is crucial for us to know and own our truths so that we can learn to ignore the lies—ones that others say about us and the ones we tell ourselves. Sometimes the lies we tell ourselves are things others have told us in the past. Those lies then become the ones we tell ourselves. Some of these lies can be traced back as far as our childhoods. They are the "you cant's," or "you will never," or "you're not __________ enough to __________."

At times it's also how certain people make us feel when we are in their presence. They seem to have no problem complimenting everyone else around us. They make us feel **"less than."** And the sad thing is we believe them. They might say things like: "Oh, your sister is so pretty" or "Oh, your friend is so smart" when in fact you are the one who is **"more than."**

*

KNOW YOUR VALUE?

Knowing your value and self-worth is just as important as owning your truth because some people will try to de-value you. What you have to remember is, some people love to tear others down, instead of lifting them up, and some will try to kick you further down from where you are.

Sometimes you may even find the same people who you'd help during their difficulties—the ones who are supposed to love, support, and protect you will forget that you helped them in the past. Some might even love it when you fail because they themselves feel inadequate, and now they have company.

When you know your value, do not let anyone "buy" you for less than you're worth, and do not shrink so that other people can feel better, and do not conform to an image that others think you ought to have. You can compromise, but do not conform. Just be true to yourself and keep believing in YOU. As I've said before, we must never be afraid to stare down our own truths and acknowledge the ones we care to own. No matter what your truth is, you can fix the ones you care to correct and move on. Do not dwell on the past. Learn and grow from it. Remember that you've got things to do, places to go, and many people to see. Keep rising!

*

SURROUND YOURSELF WITH POSITIVE PEOPLE

As you're trying to make positive changes in your life, it is important that you pay close attention to the people you surround yourself with. Are they heading somewhere? It's essential that you remain focused, faithful, fearless, and energized.

There is a saying that says something like this: **"Show me who your friends are, and I'll show you who you are."**

So, be mindful about the company you keep. You can learn a lot from successful people versus the unsuccessful ones. If you want to see *real* progress, hang with people who are positive and uplifting, and try your best to stay away from the negative ones. The latter will drag you down and try to keep you down.

• •

**If you want to see *real* progress,
hang with people who are positive
and uplifting.**

• •

*

As I'd mentioned previously, I was a bit of a perfectionist. Over the years, I'd start writing, and then I'd stop. Rewrite. Start and stop. Rewrite. Start and stop. I kept beating myself up because I knew how to set and smash goals. I've crushed a few before. I went to school and got a decent education. I worked hard. I've had some great jobs. I've built two homes from the ground up. The first one I bought at the age of twenty-six (and single, I might add). I took great pleasure in picking out the model of the home I wanted, the cabinets, the flooring, the lighting and everything else in between. When I moved into that house, I had everything that I could possibly need for that home, from brand new furniture right down to the silverware.

It's a special feeling when you find out that you are approved for a big loan from a lending institute. It usually means that you are on the right track—that you must be doing some things right.

This is where I should give credit to my mom, who has set a good example for me to follow—to set my goals, make a plan, and go after what I want relentlessly.

I was well on my way with my savings and investments and was still able to sneak a vacation in here and there.

I could afford to go out to lunch or dinner with friends. You could say that I had everything going for me. I was at the point of living my life, thinking that I'm not going to waste my time on "any" man; if the right one comes along, great! But I wasn't about to "settle" just to have a man.

I eventually met and married a decent man (we built the second home together). When my husband entered my life a few years later, I had my first home and a brand-new car to boot.

I'd started a business from scratch and worked hard to move from zero to a highly profitable state.

I now have two kids who are the joy of my life.

You could say that I've always been a go-getter. My list of accomplishments could go on. Now, don't get me wrong here, I'm far from perfect. I've had my share of mistakes and failures.

I've experienced the loss of a business and the loss of loved ones. I've suffered disappointments, setbacks, and betrayals. But I'm still standing—flawed, but I'm still here!

As I move on to the next stage, I know that if I want to design the life I want, I have to keep moving.

Let me tell you also that it's never too late to start. Unless you begin, you'll never know where your story might end. Sometimes we put our lives on hold, waiting for the perfect time to make a move. We want to wait until we have more money or more time. We want to wait until the kids get older or when we retire, or we want to wait until we're healthier, et cetera, before we take our next steps.

I've decided that I don't want to look back on my life and have too many regrets. When I look back, I don't want to see too many missed opportunities or, worse, that I did not wholeheartedly pursue my goals and dreams. I don't want that for myself, and I hope you don't want that for yourself either.

I've decided that I'd make a conscious decision to let go of my fears, doubts, worries, and hang-ups and start doing the *one thing* that I've been dreaming about for some time, and you can too.

BELIEVE that you have the power to move forward from where you are, starting right at this moment.

Whatever you do, do not quit! Find the strength and courage to persist, no matter what. Believe that you can do what you think you can do; trust that everything will work out eventually.

CHAPTER 7

WHAT DOES SUCCESS MEAN TO YOU?

*It doesn't matter where you come from, what you have or
don't have, what you lack, or what you have too much of.
But all you need to have is faith in God, an undying passion
for what you do and what you choose to do in this life, and
a relentless drive and the will to do whatever it takes to be
successful in whatever you put your mind to.*

- STEPHEN CURRY-

* * *

Time and time again we've heard stories about everyday people
who are living their grandest dreams despite the odds that were
stacked up against them. How did they blast through their fears,
self-doubts, and other negative emotions to create the life they
now have?

There is no doubt that for many of these people to
succeed they would have had to think and do things differently,
but how did they get to that point?

What ultimately drove them to success?

Perhaps when you think of super successful people,
certain ones might appear in your mind. However, when I think
of these people, my list would include Oprah Winfrey, J.K.

Rowling, Steve Jobs, Bill Gates, Elon Musk, Mark Zuckerberg, Sir Richard Branson, Warren Buffet, Shonda Rhimes, Anthony Robbins, Tyler Perry, Barbara Corcoran, Mark Cuban, and Dwayne Johnson.

These "special" people have inspired me over the years in many different ways. Each has changed our world in unique ways. Some of these people have passed on, but the thing I love the most is that even though some may have passed on, their legacies still live on.

When I looked into the backgrounds of some of these super successful people, I found many didn't set out to become extraordinary. They became extraordinary because they had a vision for their lives even though those visions might not have been crystal clear from the beginning.

Take a moment to ponder what you've read so far, then answer the following questions before you go any further.

QUESTIONS:

- Which super successful people inspire you the most, and why do they? (List the names of at least three people.)

____

____

- How many of the people who inspire you are on the world stage today?

  ____

  ____

- Would you be able to find any successful or super successful people in your backyard?

  ____

  ____

- What can you learn from some of these successful, super successful, or extraordinary people? (Make a list of all the things you think you'd want to learn about.)

  ____

  ____

  ____

SOMETHING TO THINK ABOUT:

Keep thinking about the people you listed above. Find out more about them, and use their stories to motivate you as you move forward. Would you be able to make a connection with any of them?

*

HOW DO YOU DEFINE SUCCESS?

What does success mean to you? Can you easily define it?

Success might mean different things to different people. Some people might desire "big" things, while some may want more modest things. No matter what your desires are on the scale of "want," if you are at the stage where you desire to make changes in your life, it is essential that you work on developing a clear vision of what it is that you want to accomplish. Once your vision is clear, you can then take some time to plan your strategies and implement the appropriate steps to move forward.

More details on how to develop a stronger vision will be provided later in Chapter 11.

• •

**Success might mean different things
to different people.**

• •

*

UNDERSTANDING YOUR WHYS

For you to move from where you are to where you want to be, it is critical that you understand why you want what you want or why you want to do what you want to do.

Is your WHY important to you simply because you are passionate about that particular thing, or is it because you want to create a better life for yourself and your loved ones? Does your WHY go deeper because you have a strong desire to fulfill your life's purpose?

*

There was a time in my life where I felt lost and alone. This was shortly after I had walked away from a business that had become physically, emotionally, spiritually, and financially draining. At the time, I didn't like what I was feeling and so I went on a soul-searching journey to seek some answers to questions that had become important to me. Some of the critical questions I was asking myself were:

- *Who are you and what have you been doing with your life thus far?*

- *Are you fulfilling your life's purpose?*

It took some time, but thankfully, I was able to find answers to those questions, and since then I'm fully aware that my passion and purpose is writing.

Below are my reasons for writing:

- First, I write to honor God. He has given me a gift that I plan to use to make a difference in the lives of others. My writing has made an enormous difference in my life. I also want to leave a legacy for my children and grandchildren. I hope that one day they might find comfort in reading my thoughts and words.

- Second, I'm passionate about writing. I write because it soothes my soul.

- Third, I am earning an income from my writing, and for a busy mom, that's a BONUS!

Knowing that my true talent is writing has helped to illuminate my path. I can feel deep down within me that this is the path I should be on because it feels right. My children light my path during those moments when I want to throw myself a pity party or when I feel like going to the city center to throw a temper tantrum.

EXERCISE:

Take some time to think about your WHYs, **and then write three things that are driving you. (List the most important ones first.)**

As you work through the exercises, use the things you have identified above as your primary focus to help you identify and understand your WHYs.

Once you understand your WHYs, use them to illuminate your path going forward. You might get discouraged along the way, but if you stay focused on the people and things that motivate you, you can succeed—look to a loved one and continue to do the things that make you feel good.

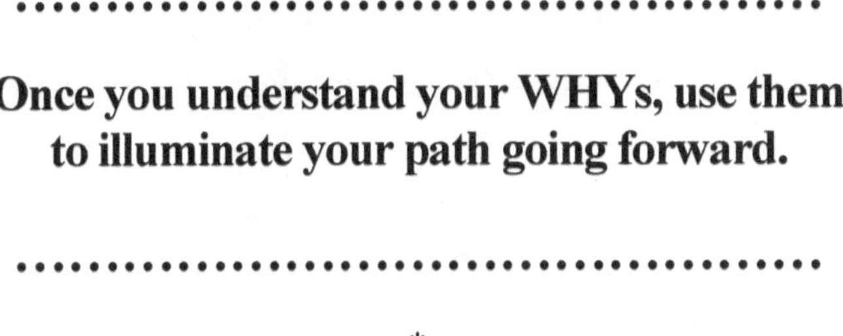

Once you understand your WHYs, use them to illuminate your path going forward.

*

LIVING A PURPOSEFUL LIFE

If you haven't yet figured out what your purpose is, I recommend that you do this as soon as you get the first opportunity to do so. Some people often get in a tizzy when we talk about finding our purposes or when we talk about focusing on doing the *one thing* that we're passionate about. If you tend to get into a tizzy or become uncomfortable about this topic, I'd like to ask you to humor me for just a bit. Now, breathe in, exhale, and keep an open mind as you continue to read.

Although it may not always be economically viable for us to monetize our passion, I believe that we will never be able to find complete happiness and contentment until we begin to use our God-given talent, one way or the other. If you are not convinced, take a look at Mother Teresa, Walt Disney, Dr. Phil, and Oprah. They are good examples of people who have used their talents to make a difference. That's what I call purposeful living!

*

Some people might realize at some point that their lives are unfulfilled and lack meaning and purpose. They will persist in the search, and often will find their purpose. And when they do, they will become unstoppable. Unfortunately, some people never seek to find their purpose.

Where do you fit it?

Do you care to know what your purpose is, or are you already on track to living a purposeful and meaningful life?

*

A PLACE TO START

A good place to begin searching for your purpose, if this is the case, is to ask yourself the following questions:

- What is the reason for my existence?

- What am I good at?

- What do I feel passionate about?

- Am I living the life of my dreams (or at least striving to create the life I want)?

- Am I happy, fulfilled, and content (or what will make me happy, fulfilled, and content)?

- What can I do to make a difference in the world?

If you already know what your talent is, do you believe you're using it to do "good" in this world? Mother Teresa believes that each of us can make a difference—just a small drop in the ocean.

*

Rick Warren offers some insight into one's life purpose when he says: "It is not about you. The purpose of your life is greater than your own personal fulfillment, your peace of mind, or even your happiness. It's far greater than your family, your career, or even your wildest dreams and ambitions. If you want to know why you were placed on this planet, you must begin with God. You were born *by* his purpose and *for* his purpose."

In his book *Self Matters*, Dr. Phil McGraw says: "When chores, routine existence, and just playing it safe become the only purpose in life, there is no purpose, and one must be found. You *need* to know your "highest and best use" in this world, and then to pursue it. How tragic would it have been if Einstein had spent his life as a merchant or a sailor; if Elvis had remained a truck driver; if Mother Teresa had been an accountant or a waitress?"

After knowing about Tony Robbins' and Brian Tracy's stories, I think it would be sad if they hadn't reached higher. As mentioned at the beginning of this book, Tony was a former janitor, and Brian worked in laboring jobs. Thankfully both knew deep down that they were capable of accomplishing significant things.

Dr. Myles Munroe, the author of *The Principles and Power of Vision,* says: "The problem is that most people have no vision beyond their current circumstances. Without a vision of the future, life loses its meaning. An absence of meaning then leads to a lack of hope. Whenever people are hopeless about their life situations, they can become resentful of their jobs or families. They feel as if they are wasting their lives, and they start living with a vague but constant internal longing for something more."

The following verse encourages us to do something positive with our lives.

Whatever your hand finds to do, do it with all your might.

Ecclesiastes 9:10

CHAPTER 8

KEEP TRUSTING

Our heavenly Father understands our disappointment, suffering, pain, fear, and doubt. He is always there to encourage our hearts and help us understand that He's sufficient for all of our needs.

- CHARLES STANLEY -

* * *

Many of us have been at a point in our lives when we want to do something but we become crippled by fear. We want to make a move, but we worry that we may not be good enough, pretty enough, or smart enough to do the "thing" that we want to do the most.

Robert H. Schuller said: "If you listen to your fears, you will die never knowing what a great person you might have been."

The good news is some of us have managed to garner enough confidence to work through our doubts, fears, and worries and have moved on to live happier, healthier, wealthier, and more productive and fulfilled lives.

Unfortunately, some of us are still stuck in the same position we've been in for some time because we lack the courage and confidence to move forward progressively. A tell-tale sign, for example, is the book we started to write two years ago remains unfinished; we might have made significant progress but got hung up on a simple thing that we haven't been able to move past.

The "masterpiece" painting is still sitting on the easel in the exact spot we left it months ago, and we haven't done anything with the business idea we were sure would be the next Facebook, Amazon, or Uber success story. Needless to say, our bank accounts remain the same and, in some cases, worse because our income levels seem to be at a standstill, while the cost of living, especially here in North America, keeps increasing. Many people are working extremely hard, yet they're struggling to make ends meet, living from paycheck to paycheck.

Okay, perhaps your situation isn't as drastic as what I've described above. However, if you're currently at the point where your fears are holding you hostage, then I want to reiterate that you are not alone. I'm an example of someone who has pushed past self-doubts, fears, and worries. I am more than aware that I'm in control of my life, and so, I'm focusing on doing the things I know deep down I should be doing. I hope you will always strive to do the same.

Below is another excerpt from *It's All Up to YOU*:

> "There is no doubt that sometimes it can be difficult for us to stay on track with creating the ideal lives we want for ourselves, especially when we have so much on our plates. Chances

are some of us have had to deal with the harsh reality of life, and so it goes: we get a job, get married, purchase a home or have kids, and our dreams and desires either get delayed or, worse, forgotten. In the worst-case scenario, we might have had to deal with disappointments, setbacks, and losses. Before we know it, we are at a particular stage in our lives, and we're dissatisfied with the way things have turned out. Somehow we do not feel happy, connected, and fulfilled. We're wondering what is next."

*

DON'T WORRY ABOUT THE LITTLE THINGS

I believe many of us can look back on moments when we had spent far too many waking hours worrying about a particular challenge or situation that we might have been in, and today we'd wonder why we did that. Some of the lyrics in one of Bob Marley's popular songs suggests that we don't worry because everything, even something small, is going to be okay.

These lyrics can remind us not to spend too much time worrying, especially about the little things in life. I know sometimes this is easier said than done. However, I find that a song, a quote, a kind word, or gesture can remind us to stop worrying and focus on the present. These reminders have the power to pull us right back into the moment.

I recommend you find something that will inspire you to keep pushing forward in those moments of weakness or indecisiveness. For example, you can meditate on a *Bible* scripture, a song, or quote. You can also read a good book or listen to uplifting music. No matter what, stay strong.

• •

A song, a quote, a kind word, or gesture can remind us to stop worrying and focus on the present.

• •

*

THE UNIVERSE SUPPORTS YOU

The reality is, many of us will face disappointment, setbacks, and losses at some point in our lives. When we do, it is normal for us to feel a myriad of negative emotions: sadness, anxiety, fear, anger, et cetera. When we're experiencing difficulties, it's reassuring to know we are never alone; we can trust that God is with us.

So, no matter where you've been or where you're going, keep believing in yourself and your abilities to create your *own* reality. Know that there is something at play that is much bigger than you. Yes. The Universe has your back!

The following verse can reassure us of God's goodness:

No temptation has seized you except what is common to man. And God is faithful; he will not let you be tempted beyond what you can bear. But when you are tempted, he will also provide a way out so that you can stand up under it.

- 1 Corinthians 10:13 -

*

I take great comfort in knowing that, YES, God supports my vision. All I have to do is believe, trust, breathe, and let go. The strategies and action steps I developed using the *S10S Blueprint* helped me to stay focused on my **goals** and **intentions.**

What helps me most to stay on track when I find myself worrying is having the awareness that I will never be given more than I can bear. I can trust this wholeheartedly.

• •

When we're experiencing difficulties, it's reassuring to know that we are never alone.

• •

*

TRUST THAT THINGS WILL HAPPEN ON GOD'S TIME

At times, we may get frustrated because things aren't happening as fast as we'd like them to, but what many of us should understand is that God's timetable is usually not the same as ours. Quite often while we are worrying about our problems, God is working on them for us lovingly, diligently, and silently.

We should also understand that often when we suffer hard times it is very likely that we are being prepared for something bigger and better. And once we are ready, everything will become clearer. We may even be better able to appreciate the good times, having gone through the hard times.

What's essential is we don't fall back on excuses for the circumstances that aren't going well or the timetable that's causing us frustration. We need to take control over our lives; so this means accepting responsibility for our own actions, attitudes, habits, and behaviors and learn to practice patience while we wait for God to prepare us for the plan he has been working on.

*

This story about a loved one can serve as a reminder not to worry and to trust that the Universe *truly* supports us.

This loved one suffered a back injury that prevented him from doing strenuous lifting, but finding a job in his field that didn't require heavy lifting was proving almost impossible. I remember how disappointed he was when he applied for a job at a large corporation and was turned down. Instead of getting mired down in excuses and blame, however, he persevered, and two months later, he found a job that paid him a lot more money than the other job would have paid. The best part is he was not required to do any heavy lifting, and he loves his new job!

The above is a great example for us to stop doubting, stop worrying, and just do what we know deep down in our hearts we ought to be doing, because in many cases, things will work out for the good. We've got to BELIEVE that!

*

PRACTICING GRATITUDE

I've discovered I am much happier when I make a point of acknowledging the things that I am grateful for daily. When I stop to reflect on how far I've come and the distance I still need to go, my perspective usually changes instantly. I know that I cannot get to where I want to go if I cannot acknowledge and appreciate my many blessings.

Zig Ziglar says: *"Gratitude is the healthiest of all human emotions. The more you express gratitude for what you have, the more likely you will have even more to express gratitude for."*

Yes, there is no doubt things can get difficult sometimes. However, many of us still have a lot of positive things going for us despite the bad. For example, family, friends, health, food, shelter, electricity, clean drinking water, and a job are all things we should be thankful for. We can send good vibrations back to the Universe when we show our appreciation by singing praises, praying, and saying thank you. The mere fact that we're alive and well is something to be grateful for.

So, what about you? Are you making a conscious effort to celebrate your blessings despite what may be occurring or has occurred in your life?

Take a step back and look at all the things you've accomplished in your life thus far. I think when you look back at the distance you have traveled, you'll realize that you may have a lot to be thankful for.

*

HOPE AND FAITH

During difficult times, it is important we remain hopeful and faithful because with hope and faith, anything is possible.

I believe lack of hope and faith is one of the reasons why there is so much hostility and violence in our world today. The evolving political environment, the war on terrorism, and the world's current economic affairs has added to the problems and concerns of many people. And as a result, many people are experiencing a combination of unpleasant emotions such as sadness, anxiousness, fear, and anger.

The following verse can remind us to remain hopeful.

Anyone who is among the living has hope—even a live dog is better off than a dead lion! For the living know that they will die, but the dead know nothing, they have no further reward, and even the memory of them is forgotten.

Ecclesiastes 9:4-5

CHAPTER 9

MAKE EACH DAY COUNT

"For the past 33 years, I have looked in the mirror every morning and asked myself: 'If today were the last day of my life, would I want to do what I am about to do today?' And whenever the answer has been 'No' for too many days in a row, I know I need to change something."

- STEVE JOBS -

* * *

As I've said previously, we have the power to begin transforming our lives at any moment, on any given day.

Usually, when we talk about changing our lives, it's because we want to achieve more or to become a better version of ourselves. Sometimes, wanting more isn't just about yearning for material things. Whatever *more* is depends on the individual and the goals and dreams that are important to them—whether it is to have more money or freedom, a better education, a better job, to become healthier, or to become stronger in our faith.

*

My mom left everything and everyone behind many years ago when she decided to migrate from her beautiful home country of Jamaica to seek better opportunities in Canada. She realized that she wanted "more" and knew that she couldn't achieve all that she wanted if she was to stay where she was at. My mom was smart enough to know that she couldn't help the people who she loved and cared about the most by being afraid and staying stuck living a mediocre life. So, she didn't hesitate to leave her comfort zone. She packed up what she could and headed for Canada. From this land of love, peace, and prosperity, she managed to carve out a life, where she could rise and lift many others along the way. It wasn't easy for her. This can be gleaned from the many stories she'd sometimes share about her journey and the many obstacles she'd had to overcome.

Today, my mom is a successful woman, who is stronger and wiser. She is continuing to make a difference in the lives of the many people she touches, from her family, friends, clients, and fellow church members to everyday people who she may meet as she goes about her daily endeavors. My mother's smile and constant words of love and encouragement remind me every day to keep aiming higher—no matter how many hurdles I have to burst through—to be confident, courageous, and persistent. Even when things don't turn out the way I'd hope, I simply have to keep moving and keep BELIEVING in the possibilities.

My mom's story, as well as the stories of many of these "special" people who had to overcome insurmountable obstacles to get to where they're at today, can inspire us all. Each of them will leave an indelible handprint on our world.

My mom's legacy and story of love, hope, and resilience will leave a huge mark on my life.

*

When I was writing *It's All Up to YOU*, I was at a stage in my life where I felt I was ready to take my life to the next level. This was after I'd spent many years building my career and then starting a couple of businesses. When my kids arrived, they became my top priority. I wanted to focus as much of my time and attention as I could into motherhood, and so I decided to make some personal sacrifices. Some of these sacrifices included some of my work, relationships, and finances.

So, for me to accomplish my goal of writing and publishing my books within a short time, it meant that I had to be laser-focused. Socializing was one of the things that had to go. I decided I'd spend a year saying no to anything that wasn't moving me closer to where I wanted to go. This is quite a contrast to Shonda Rhimes who spent a year saying yes to new opportunities and experiences. Fortunately for Shonda she had arrived at a stage in her life where she wanted to let her sleeves down a bit. Based on her book, *A Year of YES,* I think it would be fair to say that she knew she was lacking and needed to grow in specific areas. I might add that Shonda decided to say YES to things because it was more of a challenge from her sister who felt that Shonda could say yes to certain things she was saying no to—things like speaking at or attending events she was regularly being invited to.

For me, I felt that saying no would allow me to say yes to other things later. I am surprised that, for the most part, my kids have been supportive and understanding (I guess you could say I owe them for being so generous.).

A typical summer break would find us making multiple trips to amusement parks or the lake and visiting or inviting family and friends over for barbecues.

In the summer of 2016, for example, we vacationed for two weeks in Mexico. The following year, 2017, things got a little crazy, so we decided to schedule a short and fun getaway instead. Quality is usually better than quantity after all, especially when you want to focus on building your dreams.

I think Jack Canfield said it best when he said: "Successful people maintain a positive focus in life no matter what is going on around them. They stay focused on their past successes rather than their past failures, and *on the next action steps they need to take to get them closer to the fulfillment of their goals* rather than all the other distractions that life presents to them."

• •

Believe that you have the power to transform your life at any moment, on any given day.

• •

*

HOW DISTRACTED ARE YOU?

So just how distracted are you? Considering we live in such a busy and overwhelming world, it's understandable that it can be difficult for many of us to stay on track with our goals. With social media, telephone, and other technology readily available, we tend to become easily distracted. The world's economic and political affairs also play a significant role in the reason why we've become so distracted, and this often may find us glued to our television on most evenings, merely to find out about the latest political and other antics, incidents, or disasters that might have occurred.

Although, it's usually a good idea for us to be aware of the events that are occurring around us, it's also essential that we learn to unplug from distractions from time to time so that we can focus on doing the things we need to do in a more productive and meaningful way.

May I suggest you take a look at Jack Canfield's quote above one more time and zoom in on: *"and on the next action steps they need to take to get them closer to the fulfillment of their goals."*

So, how distracted are you? Are you focusing on your priorities? Like Steve Jobs, are you looking in the mirror every morning and asking: *"If today were the last day of my life, would I want to do what I am about to do today?"* If your answer is "No," then I hope you are at the point where you're willing to start making positive changes.

. . . .

It's essential that we unplug from distractions from time to time.

. . . .

*

BELIEVE IN YOURSELF AND YOUR ABILITIES

Having confidence in yourself is critical. We can't win big if we cannot demonstrate that we're confident. If other people see us wobbling, then how can they trust us to lead or do something that's important?

Sometimes it's the *"Yes, I can"* moments that will give us the strength to propel ourselves forward. So, keep telling yourself that you can, even when things might seem impossible.

*

EXAMPLES OF INSPIRING PEOPLE

If you are at the stage in your life where you want to make significant changes, just try to focus on your dreams and goals, and BELIEVE in the possibilities. Know that you can succeed despite your past, doubts, fears, or worries. It's important to remember that many people had experienced moments in their lives when they decided to aim higher, and through hard work and determination, they became super successful.

Tony Robbins, Brian Tracy, Tyler Perry, J.K. Rowling, Shonda Rhimes, and Sir Richard Branson are excellent examples of people who have transformed their lives in incredible ways.

Sir Richard Branson, one of the world's richest men, experienced amazing transformation. He had dyslexia and performed poorly in school and was told by the headmaster that he would either end up in prison or become a millionaire. He chose the latter. He eventually dropped out of school at the age of fifteen and moved on to start multiple ventures, including Virgin Records and Virgin Atlantic Airlines. Branson made a wise choice by turning his life around full circle. He is now a billionaire, but more importantly, he is using his story to inspire many others to make positive changes. Now, how about that?

Shonda Rhimes, who has succeeded tremendously as a writer for hit TV shows like *Grey's Anatomy, Scandal,* and *How to Get Away with Murder,* came from a middle-class background and experienced financial difficulties during her college years. In her bestselling book, *The Year of YES,* Shonda wrote about her prior struggle between choosing to purchase a bottle of wine or things like toilet paper because at times she couldn't afford to buy both. Shonda succeeded by working hard, letting go of her fears, and embracing her idiosyncrasies. Shonda is an outside the box thinker. It is that difference that, I believe, sets her apart from many writers.

Tyler Perry is someone who rose from rags to riches after spending many years pursuing his writing and show business career. Tyler said he succeeded because of God's grace. In a YouTube video, Tyler advised his fans to keep planting their seeds, keep watering them, and keep BELIEVING.

Tyler further urged us not to spread our water over too many seeds. He said we should make our idea a priority. When we know it's the right thing to focus on, we'll feel it deep down—we will know it beyond knowing it because that "thing" will never allow us to let it go. That thing will keep us going even when we can't keep ourselves going. Tyler said he did not stop believing in his dream. All he wanted to do was one show. In 1992 Tyler organized his first show and was expecting to have approximately twelve hundred attendees, but only around thirty showed up, and these were mostly friends and family members. He did it again in 1993, 1994, 1995, 1996, 1997, and 1998, and he got the same results—only about thirty people would show. Eventually, things got better, and people began to take notice. Tyler kept going and as a result became super successful. It is reported that he has a net worth that is estimated to be at six hundred million dollars. What I love the most about Tyler's story is that he never gave up when things didn't turn out the way he'd expected them to. I believe many of us would have given up on the third or fourth attempt.

What sticks in my mind the most is that because Tyler felt deep down that he was on the right track he persisted. This is a lesson for many of us; again, if we think that we're on the right track, we should keep moving forward because eventually we'll achieve or exceed the results we want.

J.K. Rowling, who is best known for her Harry Potter book series, rose from rags to riches to become one of the world's richest women. Rowling said since she was around five or six she wanted to become a writer. And that was the one thing she BELIEVED—that she was a storyteller. She had written over the years but didn't find the right thing up until the age of twenty-five when the idea for the first Harry Potter novel popped into her head.

Among other achievements, *Time Magazine* named Rowling as a runner-up for its 2007 Person of the Year, and in 2010, she was named the "Most Influential Woman in Britain".[3]

Dwayne Johnson had no idea that being cut from the CFL would lead him to a successful wrestling and acting career. As I've mentioned before, Dwayne wanted to play in the NFL, but his dream was shattered when he was injured playing football in college. He made his way to the CFL after college with hopes that he could heal and improve so he could have a better chance of playing in the NFL. However, shortly after his arrival to the CFL, he was cut from that league too. Johnson was devastated but somehow managed to pick himself up to become super successful, first in the WWE and then as an actor. I'm sure Dwayne had doubts and worries; however, he managed to pick himself up from where he was.

Oprah Winfrey knew at a young age she wouldn't be hanging other people's laundry to dry when her grandmother asked her to pay attention because one day she might have to

---

[3] You can learn more about J.K. Rowling at:
https://en.wikipedia.org/wiki/J._K._Rowling or other online resources, including www.Youtube.com

do the same for a living. Oprah knew she would not be doing *that*. Over the years, Oprah had doubts and worries, but she didn't let those stop her—she kept moving through disappointments, countless betrayals, and other challenges. We can say here that the rest is history!

Oprah thought she could and she did, and look where her path led her!

CHAPTER 10

STOP AIMING FOR PERFECTION

"Perfection to me is, I walk away from a situation and say, 'I did everything I could do right there. There was nothing more that I could do."

- DRAKE -

* * *

Don't aim for perfection, simply do the best you can at anything you may do, and then let it fly. You just might be amazed at how far you may get once you start and keep going.

There were numerous times when I came close to not publishing my previous book at the time I did. Despite having combed through the book numerous times, I kept asking myself if it was ready—if it was the best book I could write. Toward the end of the publishing process, I remember waking up one morning with a serious panic attack because I was freaking out about whether a reader would find any erroneous errors or typos in it.

Now, deep down I knew that if there were a few errors or typos (and there is bound to be a few) that a "reasonable" reader would ignore them if the overall quality of the book is good. I've read many great books that have typos in them. In fact, a couple of months after my book was published, I began reading Tim Ferris's bestselling book *The 4-Hour Workweek* which was published in 2007 and revised and expanded in 2009; in this book, Tim wrote: *"This is not a "revised" edition in the sense that the original no longer works. The typos and small mistakes have been fixed over 40 printings in the U.S. This is the first major over-haul, but not for the reason you'd expect."* Tim went on to further explain he revised and expanded this book because things have changed. He said *"Things have changed dramatically since April 2007. Banks are failing, retirement and pension funds are evaporating, and jobs are being lost at record rates."*

Now, what I want to emphasize here is despite the errors and typos, at the time of writing the revised version, *The 4-Hour Workweek* had been sold in thirty-five languages and was on the bestseller lists for more than two years. So there I was worried about my *little* book. If Tim's book had errors but still went on to become so popular, then there was a bit of hope for mine. At the time of writing this book you are now reading, *The 4-Hour Workweek* is still an Amazon bestseller. Seriously! This goes to show that, in many cases, we should spend less time doubting and worrying and just focus on **doing** the things we know we ought to be doing. Now, this doesn't mean we shouldn't put our best effort into doing whatever it is we're doing. **This simply means that at some point we'll have to bring some things to a conclusion, whether it's our day-to-day activities or a special project that we've been working on.** If we are to make progress, we ought to keep moving forward in a timely manner.

*

DON'T DIE ON A SMALL HILL

While you're focusing on the things that truly matter—the ones that will make a significant difference in your progress—**are there some things that you could let slide, for just a bit?**

I believe that we shouldn't die on small hills, meaning let's not spend too much time worrying about the little things in life. For example: When I want to focus on my writing or meet a deadline, my home tends to look like a bomb had exploded inside. It's a huge adjustment for me, but I've told myself a super clean home cannot pay my bills. I have to save my energy for bigger, more important things. I know I also have to take better care of myself.

Now, remember that this is coming from someone who once strived for perfection; however, as I've said before, in many cases, ***done is better than perfect!*** I've realized that I cannot get very far in accomplishing my major life goals if everything is neatly kept together at all times. If I strive too hard for perfection, I'm either going to drive my family crazier than they already are or I'm going to have a nervous breakdown. I've decided that neither will be worth it.

Developing this mentality has allowed me to have more "me" time—with no guilt, apologies, or excuses. Well, perhaps just a bit (Here comes another smiley emoji.).

*

PRACTICING SELF-CARE

Although we may want to use our time wisely while we focus on our major life goals, it is even more important that we practice to take better care of ourselves. This means that sometimes it is critical that we put our emotional and physical needs ahead of the needs of others. Many of us were taught that it is selfish to put ourselves first, but that's not quite true, especially when portraying our "good" self would benefit the people around us.

Mothers in particular tend to put their family's needs ahead of their own. We feel guilty taking time out for ourselves. Being a mom of two children, I must admit that I am guilty at times of not taking care of myself when I really should. I have a tendency to keep going even when I am ill or fatigued because there seems to be a never-ending list of things to do around the house.

Taking time out for ourselves will not only help us to recharge but also to refocus on our goals and intentions. When those are clear to us, we will be more emotionally ready to help others. Let's face it, even the Energizer Bunny is going to run out of steam at some point, and its batteries are going to have to be replenished.

If you practice taking time for yourself, putting yourself first when you need to, and giving love to yourself, you'll have more love and attention to pass on to others when the right time comes.

Now for some questions: **When was the last time you did something special for *you*?**

Perhaps now would be a good time to purchase that beautiful coat you've always wanted. Or, how about treating yourself to a nice lunch or dinner or a professional massage, manicure, or pedicure?

Take some time to think about what you can do for **YOU**!

• •

Sometimes it is critical that we put *our* emotional needs ahead of the needs of others.

• •

*

LIVING IN THE MOMENT

Since I've written about the importance of practicing proper self-care, I think it is equally essential that we make adequate use of the present time and make conscious choices as we move forward. We truly do have the power to create the present, so we should remain focused on doing the things we have to do for ourselves and the people who are present in our midst. Living in the past will only bring us the same unhappiness that the past itself brought us.

To fully move on and create the person you want to be and the life you want to live, do everything possible to live in the present—including using affirmations to emphasize affirmative action and taking time for yourself to enjoy the moment, no matter how fleeting it might be.

While it's great to think and plan for the future, it is wise that we don't overthink things. Doing so may cause us unnecessary stress and angst. It's always a good idea to try to remain calm and collected as we move forward from any situation or predicament that we may find ourselves in.

EXERCISE:

Now that you've had some time to reflect, can you identify some of the things that are of the utmost importance? If you can, then list them below:

____

____

____

____

What are some of the things that you could let slide a bit?
List them below:

____

____

____

____

CHAPTER 11

FOCUS ON WHAT YOU WANT

Thoughts become things. If you see it in your mind, you will hold it in your hand.

- BOB PROCTOR -

* * *

The key is never to stop thinking about all the things you want to achieve. *The Secret* states: "The only reason why people do not have what they want is that they are thinking more about what they don't want than what they do want. Listen to your thoughts, and listen to the words you are saying."

As you move forward, pay close attention to the things you're focusing on. Are they positive or negative? Thinking about the things or experiences you want will motivate you to continue to do the things that are necessary to get the results you want to achieve, even if it means that you try to do something a different way at a different time. You will feel empowered and upbeat when you feed yourself positive thoughts!

Keep focusing on your **goals** and **intentions**. Reflect on:

- The type of house you want to live in.

- The kind of cars you want to drive.

- The places you want to travel to.

- The restaurants you want to eat at.

- Your retirement plans, your relationships, and any other experiences or things you may desire.

*

OUR LIFE WHEELS

Some experts, teachers, philosophers, and spiritual leaders believe there are seven major areas in our wheel of life, and all are essential if we are to live a fulfilled and meaningful life. So, there are specific times in our lives, whether daily, weekly, or monthly when we may need to set aside some time to focus on our intentions in these different areas. Although some people may name the following slightly differently, our wheel of life is:

1. Spiritual & Personal Development (Faith)

2. Relationships (Family & Friends)

3. Health (Fitness)

4. Work (Job or Business)

5. Money (Finances)

6. Recreation & Lifestyle (Fun)

7. Contribution (Charity)

*

GOALS VERSUS INTENTIONS

The difference between intentions and goals are subtle. **Goals** are generally more specific than intentions and have a deadline for completion. **Intentions** are vaguer and less time-sensitive than goals. Both are important to help us to achieve our dreams and desires.

Linda Francis and Gary Zukav, authors of *The Mind of the Soul*, say: *"Intention is the difference between having a vision and bringing it into the world. Inspiration is common, but inspired action is rare. The insight that illuminates a moment in the shower or occupies your thoughts while you daydream has no effect upon you or others, but using your idea or applying your insight does. The difference is intention."*

It is wise to think about our intentions before we act or react. Once we decide to pay close attention to our intentions, we can then move forward to begin living the life we were meant to live.

*

DON'T BE AFRAID TO ASK FOR SUPPORT

Sometimes for us to get to where we want to be, we might need to ask others for help or support. Often, we'll find that the others around are more than willing to support us anyway. All we simply have to do is reach out or ask.

While you hold your head down, who in your circle could you ask for help, support, guidance, patience, and understanding?

Don't forget to include your spouse and children into your plan (if applicable), and explain how they can assist and why you won't always be available to fulfill some of their needs.

*

LISTEN TO YOUR INTUITION

As you move forward, don't forget how important it is that you listen carefully to your intuition because it's usually right—it's a gift from God.

Again, if you feel that you're on the right track, keep moving. **If something doesn't feel right, then perhaps it's a sign to stop and pay attention.**

Oprah is a big believer of listening to one's intuition. Paying attention to her authentic power has been a huge part of her success. She has said that she started out on her career by listening to what felt like the truth to her.

*

DON'T BE AFRAID TO SAY "NO"

As you work toward your endeavors, I cannot stress enough how critical it is that you remain focused, especially if you already have a busy and hectic lifestyle. So, there will be times when we might need to say *no* to our families and friends, as uncomfortable as it might be to utter this powerful word to the people we love and care about. However, not being able to say "no, I cannot help you at this time" or "no, this isn't the direction I want to go" or "no, this is not my responsibility" can stand in the way of us achieving our goals.

Not only should you practice saying no to others, but more importantly, say no to yourself when you realize you are saying yes to something or someone you shouldn't. Try to save your yeses for more important situations. You can maintain control of your life at certain times when you are aware of how you need to prepare or react to certain situations. There are many other times when it is okay to say no. When you are tempted to say yes to something you feel you should be saying no to, think again, long and hard. If after thinking about it, you still feel that saying no is the right thing to do, then say it with no apologies, excuses, or guilt.

*

BE WHO YOU ARE

Lately, I've been thinking about how, as a society, many women feel as though they have to change who they are to fit in continually. We often feel the need to conform to our workplaces, churches and any other group that we may find ourselves with. We conform to our marriages and to motherhood. We are constantly thinking about others, and we often put their needs and feelings ahead of ours.

And in many cases, we seek approval for how we look or make excuses for how we act or react. I guess this is because we don't want to embarrass our family and friends. Oh, the pressure many of us are under! I'm writing this part based on my experience because my life, my priorities, and my thinking had changed over the years after my children entered my life. For a while, their needs were my main priority. They are now typical teenagers, and boy, they do get embarrassed easily. When they are around their friends, I am required to be seen and not heard, for fear that I might say something that is embarrassing or just plain not cool.

I've decided that I'll try, to a certain point, not to embarrass my kids; however, if I see or hear anything that requires me to say something or correct them, you can bet your bottom dollar that I'm going to. Likewise, if I see or hear something that I know deep down I need to address, while I'm trotting around this earth, the same will apply.

I will also speak up in my marriage and relationships whenever and wherever I feel it's necessary.

I plan to maintain some of the spirits I had during my youth—that fearless, fun, and hopeful spirit.

I recently picked up a copy of Brene Brown's recent book, *Braving the Wilderness*. As I was flipping through the pages, the following piece caught my attention (I think it's worth sharing. It's also a book that I think you might want to add to your collection, depending on your interests.):

> When we commit to getting closer, we're committing to eventually experiencing real, face-to-face conflict. Whether it's over dinner, at work, or in the grocery line, in-person conflict is always hard and uncomfortable. And when it comes to family—it's even harder and more painful.[4]

Brene went on to say further:

> Maintaining the courage to stand alone when necessary in the midst of family or community or angry strangers feels like an untamed wilderness. When I get to the point where I'm like.......*It's just too hard. I'm too lost!* I hear Maya Angelou's words again: *The price is high. The reward is great.*[5]

Yes. Conflicts can be hard and uncomfortable. The price is high, but the reward is great!

---

[4] Page 80, Braving the Wilderness by Brene Brown, copyright @ 2017
[5] Page 80, Braving the Wilderness by Brene Brown, copyright @ 2017

CHAPTER 12

START WITH 10 SUCCESS BLUEPRINT

The key to forming good habits is to make them part of your rituals. I have a morning ritual, afternoon ritual, and Sunday ritual. It's one way to bundle good habits into regular times that you set aside to prepare yourself for the life you want. Rituals help you form habits.

- LEWIS HOWES -

* * *

In the previous pages of this book, I promised to provide more details on the *S10S Blueprint* I had developed by fluke (Note that this blueprint is a work in progress.). It is designed to give you the kick-start that you might need to begin creating the life you want. You can start from where you are today, and work your way up to where you want to go in the areas you wish to see improvements.

I created this blueprint using the number ten because I believe the number ten is a number that's easy to remember and work with.

You can set and work on your goals ten minutes at a time—or set your goals list so you can focus on identifying ten goals that you'd like to achieve—for example.

Start with ten minutes, and then you can choose the top three or five goals that are most important to you. If it's your desire to start saving, you can start by saving just ten dollars each day or week.

Of course, you can increase the amount of time, money, or other things you may want to accomplish once you've gained some momentum.

Once you have gained some momentum, it is critical that you do __NOT__ stop—**keep moving.** You'll find that once you start creating good habits and routines, your mind will begin to shift, and you will begin to feel great as you begin to see your accomplishments.

When you become more conscious about the *S10S Blueprint*, you may find yourself asking questions like:

- Why am I not focusing on doing something more important at this moment?

- Is this purchase necessary (For example, do I really need another pair of shoes or a purse)?

- Do I need to eat out tonight or could I prepare a simple meal at home instead?

Remember that small changes can lead to bigger ones.

The *S10S Blueprint* will help you to develop appropriate steps and strategies that align with your goals.

• •

Once you start creating good habits and routines, your mind will begin to shift.

• •

*

START SMALL WITH THE S10S BLUEPRINT

Research has shown that for us to succeed with our goals we need to develop good habits over time (thirty days or longer). Research has also shown that when we remain consistent with new habits, they will then become routines. The *S10S Blueprint* activities are designed to be completed on a daily, weekly, or monthly basis, depending on what you want to achieve. For example:

- If you want to lose weight, it would be a good idea to design a healthy eating and exercise plan that you could implement on a daily basis. You could start with ten push-ups, ten sit-ups, ten lunges, and ten arm curls. You could then add other routines and increase these repetitions as you progress.

  You could also start walking or jogging for ten minutes, and then work your way up. If your goal is to become more organized at home or at the office, for example, you could develop specific strategies to focus on organizing that area for ten minutes each day. A great example might be to spend ten minutes after dinner to clean and organize your kitchen so that you're more prepared to begin your next day effortlessly.

- You could apply the same thinking to meditating if your desire is to become more mindful.

· ·

Strive to remain consistent with new habits for thirty days or longer.

· ·

*

GET ORGANIZED AND EFFECTIVE WITH START WITH 10

Start with ten minutes and before long you should have no problem increasing it to twenty minutes, thirty minutes, or longer, depending on what it is you'd like to achieve.

Here are some examples of how you can use the *Start with 10 Success Blueprint* to get more organized and effective in your work and home life:

- If you are consistently late for work and want to change your habit, you could spend ten minutes the night before to organize things so your mornings are not so chaotic.

You can determine how you want to organize your mornings by thinking about the things you typically spend the first ten minutes doing each day. For example, do you find yourself stacking the dishwasher or wiping the kitchen counter? Do you find yourself trying to decide what to wear to work?

Once you know what activities are eating up your mornings, then consider doing those activities the night before. For example:

- o You could tidy your kitchen so everything is clean and ready to go for breakfast the next day.

- o You could prep your breakfast ingredients or pack your lunch for the next day.

- o You could set up your coffee pot so all you have to do is press a button, and presto, coffee is ready to go on the way out the door.

- o You could pick out your outfit and organize all your take-a-longs for the next day.

Bonus: If you make your coffee at home versus spending ten minutes waiting in line at the coffee shop, you'll save yourself some time and a couple of dollars to stash away in your savings account—ten dollars or more each week. Now, you'll be winning with having more time and money!

- If you are tired of feeling disorganized or looking flaky in your weekly meetings, you could start by designating ten minutes to review your meeting notes a day or two before your meeting. Ten minutes may not seem like a lot of time, but you'd be zeroing on the things on your to-do list that you didn't get done. The topics you discussed at the meeting would be fresher in your mind, and you'll be able to respond or contribute more meaningfully. You could be viewed more like a rock star instead of looking like a flake. And if all else fails, you would have thought about the excuses you'd have to make for not getting something on your to-do list done (I don't recommend that you make excuses for your inactions, however. I think you'll get my point.).

Bonus: Did you know that the majority of super successful people organize their schedules and review their action steps and strategies for the next day on the day or night before their scheduled activities? There's no guessing in the morning when they're awake!

Think about ways that you can use the *S10S Blueprint* effectively. Which areas of your life do you think could use some improvements? Make your determination and then *Start with 10*!

Bonus: Just so you don't keep forgetting, set an alarm or mark a reminder on your calendar.

*

GET SMARTER WITH START WITH 10

There are many people on the world stage today that you could spend some time researching. These might include some of the people you have been curious about over the years but haven't had a chance to find out more about them. If you've ever wondered how these people became who they are today, well, now might be the perfect opportunity to immerse yourself into learning more about them. Learn about their success habits and how they overcame any obstacles they may have faced.

YouTube is a great source for watching dynamic videos. If your goal is to become a successful entrepreneur, read business articles that relate to the topics you're interested in (You can find great ones on www.inc.com or www.entrepreneur.com or www.forbes.com.).

- Never stop learning—read and study as much as you can. I'd suggest that you spend at least twenty or thirty minutes per day for the next sixty to ninety days studying about relevant people and materials. **If you've got only ten minutes, then start there!**

*

IMPROVE YOUR RELATIONSHIPS WITH START WITH 10

If you desire to improve your relationship with a parent, sibling, or child, how about setting aside ten minutes per day or a couple of times each week to reach out or spend time with that person? This is an **intention** that could significantly improve your relationships.

For example, you could take the time to get down on the floor to play with that child. You could also take this time to read or talk to this child—to find out how their day went with no distractions.

If you wish to build your relationship with a parent or sibling, you could reach out by making a quick phone call once or twice each week.

*

START SAVING AND INVESTING WITH START WITH 10

If your intention is to start saving but you just cannot seem to get started, how about making a commitment to put ten dollars per week into a savings account? It's a small amount, but if this is all you can afford to save, it's better than nothing. And at least it will get you in the right mindset. Sometimes we get off track with our goals because they are too big and unrealistic, so if big goals seem too unrealistic, start with small ones instead.

If you were consistent with your savings, in just one year, you would have saved five hundred and twenty dollars plus some interest. If you doubled your savings, you would have over one thousand dollars saved. That's a small win, especially if you are the type who usually has a zero balance in your savings or a negative balance in your checking accounts.

The idea is to increase your savings contribution from ten dollars to something that is manageable once you gain some momentum.

*

THE SUCCESS BLUEPRINT – EXERCISE #1

Start by thinking about the things on your wish list and then complete the following:

1. Write down *10 GOALS* you want to accomplish within the next *ten years*. Write down your goals in priority order, meaning that you should list your most important goals first. Example: purchase a new home or car, obtain a degree, start a business, start saving for retirement or your kids' education, et cetera. If you cannot come up with ten things, push for five.

2. Write down *10 PLACES* you would like to visit within the *next ten years*. List the places that you'd like to visit first. Now, these places do not have to include all exotic or foreign countries, which are usually big-ticket items (Of course, it will be fun and exciting to have some fantastic and exotic places on your list.). You can list places that you've always wanted to go to in your local area (or neighboring province or state) but never got a chance to. Example: a theater or a weekend getaway at a nice hotel that's located within driving distance from where you live.

3. Write down *10 THINGS* you'd love to do within the next *ten months*, ones that have always piqued your interest and would make you feel completely happy and fulfilled. Write down the things that you are extremely **passionate** about first. If you could, which ones would you do for free? You should be able to pinpoint at least one thing that would lead you to your life's purpose, if you aren't sure what it is yet.

   If you're not able to pursue any of the things you've identified on this list as a career choice, then at least try to do this activity on a regular basis, perhaps as a hobby or to volunteer for a good cause. The point is to consistently do whatever makes you feel the happiest. *It's important that we continue to do the things that feed our souls.*

4. After you have completed the list in number three above, make another list of *10 FUN THINGS* that you have done before but would like to do again. The idea is to get you to think deeper about doing some fun things while you're working on the "bigger" things.

5. Within the *next ten days*, write down *10 THINGS* that you have been putting off for a while—things you know you ought to get done.

   Examples would be: going to the doctor for your annual checkup, obtaining a life or medical insurance plan, completing a personal net worth statement, and balancing your checking account. If working on your personal finances is applicable, you could start by completing a household budget that you can stick to. Take a serious look at your finances. What do you owe?

This list could also include making a plan to visit a friend or relative whom you haven't seen in a while; volunteering at your church or local charity; doing some repairs around the house; cleaning out your closet and donating some unwanted items to a charity; and cleaning and de-cluttering your home. ***Do at least three of these ten things*** within the ***next ten days***.

This activity is designed to help you to begin your *Start with 10* goals and free your mind as you move forward. Eventually you'll gain some momentum.

You'll find that as you look outward, and start caring about others, you'll begin to feel better.

6. Within the ***next ten days***, write down ***10 THINGS*** that you are GRATEFUL for. This could include being grateful that you have a comfortable home, food on the table, running water and electricity, and good health. It could include arriving home safely, having a beloved family member or a good friend, a job that you enjoy, or being able to work at a hobby.

    Having an attitude of gratitude can immediately change your perspective from a negative to a positive one.

As you go forward, try to write down at *least three things* that you are grateful for on a daily basis.

7. Within the *next ten days*, write down *10 GOOD ATTRIBUTES* that you have. For example: are you a kind, hardworking, honest, trustworthy, loyal, enthusiastic, passionate person? Focus on your strengths, not your weaknesses. Yes, there is nothing wrong with trying to improve our weaknesses, if we choose to; however, if you focus on your strengths, you'll feel better about yourself.

8. Within the *next ten days*, write down *10 THINGS* that you are PROUD of. What are some of your major life accomplishments? Have you invested according to your plan? Did you graduate from college or university? Did you purchase a home? Do you have a great marriage or relationship? Do you have wonderful kids? How about your parenting skills?

CHAPTER 13

VISIONS AND GOALS

Success is about dedication. You may not be where you want to be or do what you want to do when you're on the journey. But you've got to be willing to have vision and foresight that leads you to an incredible end.

- USHER –

* * *

The following chapter will help you develop S.M.A.R.T. goals. I included it in my last book (Although it has been slightly revised, I believe it is worth including here.).

*

If you do not have a clear vision for yourself, I recommend that you take some time to reflect on what it is that you want to accomplish in your lifetime. What are your hopes, dreams, and desires? Once you have determined what you want your future to look like, then it will be time to design a plan that includes clear written goals to ensure that your goals are measurable and attainable. Research has shown that the people with written goals achieve significantly more things than the ones who don't.

. . . .

**Take some time to reflect on what it is that
you want to accomplish in your lifetime.**

. . . .

*

SET GOALS THAT ARE S.M.A.R.T.

Your plan should have step-by-step actions and timelines
that can easily be measured. S.M.A.R.T. means:

- S = Specific

- M = Measurable

- A = Attainable

- R = Realistic

- T = Timely

In other words, be specific; state clear objectives with a
specific timeline in which you'll achieve each goal.

To better explain the above, here is an example: *I will
purchase a home valued at $500,000.00 by July 1, 2019. To do
this, I will need to save an additional $2,000.00 per month to
bring the total down payment toward this home to $50,000.00.*

The desire to purchase a home is specific, meaning you know what it is that you want. July 1, 2019 is the timeline that you've established to purchase this home. The questions now are: Are the cost and time frame realistic? Is this goal attainable? Meaning, can you qualify for a mortgage of $450,000.00, and can you do this by July 1, 2019?

Perhaps a more realistic date would be December 31, 2019. If you determined that your goal is realistic, you could then design a plan to ensure that you attain this goal. How will you ensure that you can measure the steps to be taken?

In his book *The Success Principles: How to Get from Where You Are to Where You Want to Be*, Jack Canfield said: "To make sure a goal unleashes the power of your subconscious mind, it must meet two criteria. It must be stated in a way that you and anybody else could measure it. *I will lose 10 pounds* is not as powerful as *I will weigh 135 pounds by 5 PM on June 30*. The second is clearer because anybody can show up at 5 o'clock on June 30 and look at the reading on your scale. It will either be 135 pounds or less or not."

For example, if your plan includes purchasing a home within the next year or two, then you'll want to indicate the amount of down payment you'll need to save each month. Once you're closer to your purchase date, what steps will you take? Some of your activities would include setting dates and times to begin looking for that home of your dreams. Have you given any thought to the location or neighborhood in which you would prefer to live? What will that house look like (e.g., size, the number of bedrooms and bathrooms)?

Jack Canfield said: *"By envisioning your goals as already accomplished, it will make your subconscious creative mind work day and night to attract the activities, relationships, and groups that can help make them into a reality."*

Experts, teachers, and philosophers believe that when you set a goal, you should dream it. Some recommend that you try to feel yourself living that vision. Try to think about your vision just before you go to bed at night, and think about it again the minute you are awake in the mornings. Your energy will help to make your dream a reality. I believe this is why books such as *The Secret* and *The Law of Attraction* have been so popular.

The Law of Attraction is a law of nature. It's believed that the Universe receives our words and thoughts and reflects those words and thoughts back to us as life experience. I'll take this a step further and say that certain words can either be defeating or empowering. Strive to speak or think only the words that empower you—the ones that will move you forward in a positive direction.

When it comes to achieving your dreams, focus on only the things that you want to attract and attain. There's an old saying that warns us "to be careful what we wish for." Therefore, it's better to focus on the things that you do want instead of the things that you don't want. For example, focus on receiving money versus bills. Focus on health not sickness, focus on happiness instead of sadness, and focus on love instead of hate.

The Secret states: "The law of attraction is the law of creation." This law means you can create your own life into existence. You'll find that many experts and teachers will agree with this philosophy.

. . . .

**Focus on only the things that you
want to attract and attain.**

. . . .

*

THE SUCCESS BLUEPRINT – EXERCISE #2

Complete this exercise by choosing ten important goals from Exercise #1.

Pick your most important goals first, and focus on those. For example: If your goal is to travel to Europe or Asia within the next year, you might want to start stashing some money aside. You might also want to start researching and deciding on the places you'd like to visit while you're there.

- What's the ideal time to visit?

- Where will you stay?

- What attractions are you interested in?

- How much money will you need for this trip?

For each goal, develop the action steps and timelines that will move you closer to achieving your goals.

123

•••

Develop the action steps and timelines that will move you closer to achieving your goals.

•••

CHAPTER 14

THE POWER OF PERSISTENCE

A little more persistence, a little more effort, and what seemed hopeless failure may turn to glorious success.

- ELBERT HUBBARD –

* * *

It's true that many of us will experience difficulties. This is the harsh reality of life. However, when we are experiencing challenges, it is critical that we strive to remain persistent. Quitting is usually not an option, at least not until we have done everything we possibly can to resolve a particular situation. Sometimes some of us give up far too soon, if we had held on just one more day, or one more moment, we would have given ourselves the opportunity to find a suitable solution for our problems. If we are not getting the result that we hope for, sometimes it helps to do something differently. Try just one more time and our lives could change for the better. Again, there is a fine balance between knowing when to hold on and when to walk away, and sometimes letting go might be the best option.

*

FACING DIFFICULT CHALLENGES

Successful people don't give up easily. They remain persistent in accomplishing whatever it is they set out to do. They strive to make the right choices and decisions as they move forward in life and are not afraid to push boundaries. They strive to become better at what they do.

If you are at a point in your life and things are not going according to your plan, don't give up. Keep trying. Just give whatever it is your best shot, because at the end of the day, it's going to matter **to you** that you did everything you could. It doesn't matter whether you're working on a particular project or goal, a marriage or relationship, trying to get through school, or any other challenging situation.

Here is an excerpt of something that I wrote previously:

> When we're faced with difficult challenges, we usually have two choices: one to stay and fight to overcome whatever that particular situation is and the other to flee. For example, some of us will stay and fight for a relationship that's worth fighting for, and some will flee at the first sign of trouble. If it's a financial situation, some people will strive to work their way through that situation, even if it means making tough choices and personal sacrifices, while some will either ignore their creditors and stay stuck, flee from their responsibility by staying stuck, or, worse, give up on life altogether. If it's a

business, some people might give up on that business far too soon because they expected to obtain overnight success. There is a fine balance. While it is good to know when to walk away, giving up too soon can be detrimental to your success.

It's important that we develop an "I can and I will, never give up" attitude. A killer attitude will help us to become mentally strong, so instead of quitting, we stay the course.

In my previous book, I also shared my thoughts on how inspired I had become by Abraham Lincoln's persistency toward making positive changes despite the hardships that he had to endure. According to research, Lincoln led the United States through its Civil War, which is known to be the deadliest war in history. In doing so, Lincoln preserved the Union, abolished slavery, strengthened the federal government, and modernized the economy. Lincoln believed in changing some of the things that most of us would think impossible. Did Lincoln experience any failures? Yes, he did! Lincoln has a long list of failures and heartbreaks, and these include the loss of his job, a failed business, the death of his fiancée, a nervous breakdown, and many political defeats. However, the interesting thing is that Lincoln kept moving despite some hardships.

The following is another excerpt about becoming energized whenever I began to feel tired or overwhelmed by the many responsibilities I faced as a working mom:

Days later, as I continued to write, I'd think about Lincoln's quote and his journey toward making positive changes. I give credit to people like Lincoln and Albert Einstein (who also made mistakes) for setting the foundation for many of us to stand on. Through them, we can learn to develop an "I can and I will, never give up" attitude. As a working mom, whenever I feel like I want to throw myself a pity party or start to feel exhausted from the many demands of work and family life, I'd instantly become energized. I kept thinking about Lincoln and many other extraordinary and super successful people who have made tremendous sacrifices despite the obstacles they may have faced. I kept thinking if these people could do what they set out to do, so could I, and if I can do it, so can you. Think about it. Perhaps our intent isn't to achieve enormous goals or to become famous, but surely we can work hard at achieving or even exceeding the goals and visions we set for ourselves.

So, whatever you do, do not quit because **if you think you can, YOU can.**

CHAPTER 15

DON'T HESITATE TO STEP OUT OF YOUR COMFORT ZONE

Move out of your comfort zone. You can only grow if you are willing to feel awkward and uncomfortable when you try something new.

- BRIAN TRACY –

* * *

Leaving our comfort zones can be a difficult thing to do, but if we want to propel ourselves forward, it's essential that we do not hesitate to step out from time to time. I've heard it said before that everything that we need are outside of our comfort zones.

It's natural for us to shy away from doing the things that makes us uncomfortable. But it is when we are willing to do something that is risky that we're likely to achieve success. **We simply must learn to focus on our intentions and take calculated risks because some things are worth the discomfort.**

The story of Susan Cagle (Also known by her stage name, Susan Justice) comes to mind. Susan was born into a restrictive religious cult that prohibited her from doing the simple things that some of us take for granted. She was only allowed to read the *Bible* and other materials that were provided by the cult organization. Such an oppressive environment might have left a person feeling sad, lonely, fearful, and angry. Susan struggled with some of these negative emotions, but fortunately, at some point in her young life, Susan recognized that her life wasn't a normal one and had faith that she would gain a better life someday. Susan's passion for music and her admiration for Oprah inspired her to keep forging ahead, despite her difficulties.

At the age of twenty-one, she was able to break away from the only life she knew and moved to New York City. It was a huge risk, but Susan knew she had to take it so that she could survive with her sanity intact. Upon arriving in New York, she began singing throughout the city's subway system and has since made a name for herself around the world. Susan said singing at the subway made her feel connected—she no longer felt alone, because when she looked at all the people passing by, she realized that everyone had their *own* story to tell.

Susan didn't want to use her background as an excuse to not do anything positive with her life, and so she was determined to press on. My favorite part of Susan's story was hearing her say what made her happiest was knowing that she could walk down the streets of New York feeling completely free—something most of us in North America take for granted. Now, Susan could have chosen a destructive path, but she was smart enough to choose a more constructive one. This is a good example to show that if we believe in something or someone we can overcome any obstacles that we will face as we trudge on our life's journey.

*

Many years ago, one of the toughest decisions of my life was to come to terms with the fact that I had to return to work when my children were younger. The bottom line was that our family would not survive on just one income. It took me months before I could make the final decision to return to work. In the beginning, neither child coped well with the adjustment.

My son would start to cry as soon as we pulled up to the daycare. First, I would have to take my daughter inside, and by the end of the first week, she began to realize what was happening and would start to whimper as soon as I got to the door of her room. Then I would have to make a second trip to get my son, because it would be a wrestling match to try to get him through the doors of the daycare. He would hang on to me, legs tightly wrapped around mine, twisting and turning, while screaming loudly. I would try to untangle myself and walk away as fast as I could, afraid to let anyone see my tears. Listening to my son's screams made my heart feel as though it was being ripped from my body. I would try hard to regain my composure as I drove off, because it was important to me that no one at work knew what I was going through. I found a bit of comfort in knowing that it was the best I could do for our family at that time.

Many working moms might understand exactly how I felt. We often try to hide the guilt we feel knowing our kids would rather be with us instead of with someone else. But in today's society, it is almost impossible for a household to survive on just one income. At times, we have to do what we feel is necessary even if it means temporarily sacrificing our loved ones' emotional needs. At such times, we will try to convince ourselves that we have no other choice, and in many cases, we don't.

To make matters worse, the first week the children attended daycare, my husband also had to go out of town on business. I had to be up at 4:30 a.m. each day so I could get us all ready and out the door to be at the daycare by 7:00 a.m. This turned out to be a grueling week as our bodies tried to adjust to the new schedule. By Thursday, I was utterly exhausted. I am not sure how I survived, but somehow, by the grace of God, I did.

As the months went by, my children started to settle more into daycare. Some mornings when we got to the daycare, my daughter would reach for her caregiver with open arms and my son would walk in because he was no longer clinging to my legs. Two months later, my son would enter the daycare laughing and chatting—quite a contrast from the first two weeks. I was enjoying being back at work as well: among other things, it meant we had more money coming in. Our lives slowly began to get back on track, and the future was looking a whole lot brighter.

To keep me focused on moving forward, and not sinking back into excuses, I would often focus on doing things that brought me some pleasure. I would sometimes lie on the floor with the children and listen to our favorite music. My son loves dancing, so we would stand up to bop and sway to the rhythm of whatever music was playing. Sometimes we would lie in bed and watch TV (their favorite shows, of course), and at other times I'd read to them.

I also found comfort in surrounding myself with positive and uplifting people. I would read inspiring books and focus on positive thoughts and quotes—anything that would keep me moving in the right direction.

CHAPTER 16

END PROCRASTINATION AND KEEP AIMING FOR WHAT YOU WANT

Know the true value of time; snatch, seize, and enjoy every moment of it. No idleness, no laziness, and no procrastination: never put off till tomorrow what you can do today.

- PHILIP STANHOPE, 4TH EARL OF CHESTERFIELD –

* * *

We could save ourselves a lot of worries and anxiety later if we do the simple things that we know deep down we ought to do. **The things I'm talking about are relatively easy, in many cases, yet we procrastinate.** Although our intentions might be great, we cannot make progress unless we ACT!

Below is something that I wrote previously on procrastination.

> Sometimes it can be hard to overcome procrastination and get things done, so I'd like to share this with you: One of my former coaches, Andrew Barber-Starsky, taught me to pick three major activities that I wanted to accomplish each

week. These are the types of activities that will move you closer to your goals.

If nothing else gets done for that week, I would have accomplished some of my most significant goals. Andrew also taught me to start with the hardest and most difficult tasks first. For example, if I dread making cold calls or want to avoid talking to a particular person and I cannot designate these tasks, then I should focus on accomplishing these first. If you are in sales, this might feel familiar. You might have to obtain a huge account for your business and don't want to say or do anything that could jeopardize this opportunity, but instead of taking the leap, you keep delaying it. Or, perhaps you have an unsatisfied customer who requires your time and attention or a particular situation that you would prefer to avoid. In his book *Eat That Frog*, Brian Tracy says it best: "Your 'frog' is your biggest, most important task, the one you are more likely to procrastinate on if you don't do something about it. It is also the one task that has the greatest impact on your life and results at the moment."

So what task can you do that will have the greatest impact on your life? Remember: **Make your SOME DAY today or tomorrow, not next week, next month, or next**

year. Start building your dreams, and no matter what, make a conscious decision to keep moving!

Focusing on what we need to could mean the difference between us having to sleep under a tree or paying for a roof over our heads and our bills on time. Stop for a moment to think about your situation. Are you more than aware that you should be doing something, but yet you're hesitating or procrastinating? Do you find yourself making excuses?

Imagine this scenario: You're in the middle of having a great time, glass in hand, and conversations are in full swing. You know you're looking good, and frankly, you couldn't be happier, and then this thought appears in your mind: __________, *you idiot, you know you should be focusing on* ________. *You said you would, and it's still not done. Shame on you! Put that glass down right now, and go and get it done.* Your mood changes instantly, and that beautiful smile you were wearing turns into a plastic one, as the feelings of guilt, shame, and disgust sweep over you. You now look like one of the wax figures at Madame Tussaud's museum.

I think many of us have been in a situation where we know we should be doing something else at that moment, whether we may be at a party, shopping, watching television, idling on social media, or surfing the internet.

Have you ever found yourself doing something that you know you shouldn't be doing at the time you were doing it? It's usually not a good feeling. We all like to feel as though we're accomplishing things.

*

FOLLOW THE PATH OF LEAST RESISTANCE

Sometimes for us to get things done, we'll need to follow the path of least resistance. This means that we should look for the easier route. This might require some flexibility as we learn to maneuver under, over, or around whatever or whoever might be standing between us and our objectives.

Taking an easier route doesn't mean we should sacrifice value, quality, or our integrity. It simply means looking for the quicker route to get from Point A to Point B.

Stop and take a moment to think for a bit. Are you facing a resistance in an area of your life?

If you are not getting the results that you want, think about what you could do differently?

Don't give up. Keep trying.

IMAGINE, BELIEVE, TRUST, AND KEEP MOVING FORWARD!

*

ASK FOR WHAT YOU WANT

It can be difficult at times to ask for what we want; however, sometimes to make the changes we seek, it is essential that we put our pride and ego aside and ask for help, whether it be financial or other assistance. We may find that some of the people in our circles are more than willing to help out in any way they can; we only need to ask.

I remember many years ago when a position within one of the companies that I was working for became available. I felt that I was the ideal candidate to fill the post, so I waited patiently for the offer that never came. Instead, it was given to another one of my colleagues. I was hurt that it was never offered to me. It took me some twenty years later to realize that I had never asked to be put in that position. I was expecting my superiors to read my mind. How could they have known that I was interested in that position? Perhaps my colleague had asked for the job and got it. I didn't ask. I am now older and wiser. Lesson learned!

Sometimes we expect others to know exactly what we need, but in all fairness, they can't.

*

SET CLEAR EXPECTATIONS

Sometimes we may find ourselves in the middle of a prickly situation—a business or relationship dilemma, for example— wondering how we arrived at that moment, and it simply could be that we didn't set our expectations and state them clearly to the other party. The other party didn't have a clue about what we required because we didn't state the desired outcome that we expected from the start.

I believe that it's better to be clear and frank about what we expect from others. We'll then know by their response whether it's possible to achieve the results we want.

CHAPTER 17

FAKE IT UNTIL YOU MAKE IT

If you're trying to achieve, there will be roadblocks. I've had them; everybody has had them. But obstacles don't have to stop you. If you run into a wall, don't turn around and give up. Figure out how to climb it, go through it, or work around it.

- MICHAEL JORDAN -

* * *

We use the phrase "fake it until you make it" sometimes when we are not sure how to do a particular thing or when we talk about not feeling well. Many of us can "fake" it through a big meeting or presentation.

No matter what our situations are, it's important that we make it a point to get up, get dressed, and get on with our day as planned.

Another example of faking it might be starting a business that grew much bigger and faster than you had anticipated. You are now the big boss who everyone is looking to for direction. At some point, you might need to hire experts, but until then, what do you do? You'll have no choice but to fake it until you make it. I don't think you'd want your competitors, vendors, customers, and employees knowing that you're uncomfortable doing things that are not your strengths, would you? Sometimes, we have no choice but to do the best we can with what we have, whenever we can and wherever we can.

A few years ago, I was watching Joel Osteen who shared about how nervous he was about taking over his father's ministry. He didn't BELIEVE that he could walk in his father's shoes. He said that he pretty much had to fake his way through to the top. Take a look at where he is now. I don't think he has to fake it anymore. He seems to be doing more than alright.

Rihanna was a featured guest, on OWN, *Next Chapter* (This episode was filmed in Rihanna's hometown of Barbados.), and in her interview, Oprah asked Rihanna how she got so comfortable in her own sexual skin (*Esquire Magazine* had named Rihanna The Sexiest Woman Alive.). Oprah said Rihanna wears "it" very well. Rihanna said she had to fake it until she made it—she had to pretend that she was comfortable about her sexuality, but she was not. Rihanna felt like she had to fake it—she said she had to just go for it. [6]

Below is another excellent example of someone who had to fake it until she made it. If she can do it, then it's possible for many of us, don't you think?

*

----

[6] As seen on OWN, Next Chapter (Rihanna's interview with Oprah in Barbados) via YouTube.com

LUAN MITCHELL-ALTER WASN'T SURE IF SHE COULD, BUT SHE DID!

LuAn Mitchell-Halter's story is a great example of faking it. Whenever I think of LuAn, the word perseverance also comes to mind. LuAn survived hard times. Through strength, courage, and determination, she managed to rebuild her life after the death of her husband, Fred.

At one point, when their business was in a crisis over a family dispute, LuAn lived in a van with her husband, children, and two dogs. They were homeless because they had to sell everything, including their property, to finance a lawsuit to fight for their company. She said no one would hire her or her husband, despite their attempts to find jobs, but this terrible situation brought her and her late husband much closer together. Instead of crying about their loss, it seemed they were able to laugh more during this time, which was when her husband began talking about the dreams he had for himself and the aspiration for the business. Despite the odds, she and her late husband Fred Mitchell piloted Mitchell's Gourmet Food to tremendous success.

After Fred died, LuAn decided she would continue his dream. At first, people did not believe she would be able to pull this vision off because she lacked the required business experience; however, she soon began to prove that she was capable of achieving great success. After a while, other people began to take her seriously. She said at one point she could have sold the company and lived comfortably, but by then she had a good team of people and so she continued. LuAn and her team managed to overcome the obstacles they faced and were able to move the company to greater heights. Today, LuAn is a motivational speaker and author of several inspirational books.

LuAn often talks about how she rose from being homeless to building a multi-million-dollar company that gained her the honor of being named Canada's top woman entrepreneur of the year. Along the way, she battled for and won control of the company after Fred died in 1998, and in 2002, she sold the gourmet meat company to Schneiders Canada while remaining its chairperson. Today, you will find Mitchell's brand in many major supermarkets across Canada.

You may not be sure just how strong you are until something happens that tests your resolve. Keep moving anyway. If you think you can, YOU can. If you think you can't, well then, just fake it until you can.

*

PERSONAL AFFIRMATIONS

Affirmations can help you to let go of any negative feelings that you may be experiencing about yourself. It's a positive reinforcement that will teach you to love yourself and to give yourself permission to grow and to make changes. BELIEVE that you can create a better life for yourself and your loved ones.

Take some time to develop affirmations that will work for the areas in which you need some reinforcements. Once you develop your affirmations (you may wish to have several different ones), you can write them all out on Post-it notes or on a card and put them in places where you can reach for them if you need to throughout your day: for example, on your bathroom or dresser mirror, in your car, at your desk, or on your refrigerator door.

Affirmations usually begin with an "I am," "I can," or "I will" statement. Below are some examples:

- I am powerful, intelligent, beautiful, smart, talented

- I am capable of handling my finances in a responsible manner

- I can stop smoking, or I will stop smoking

- I am loveable, or I can learn to love better

- I am a good person, or I can be a better person

- I am emotionally healthy, or I can become emotionally healthy

- I love and accept who I am

- I am courageous, or I will face my fears courageously each day

- I am a survivor, or I will survive this difficult time

- I will lose weight, or I am healthy

- I am blessed, or I deserve to enjoy the fruits of my labor

Spend a few minutes each day (preferably in the morning and at night before you go to bed) to focus on your affirmations. Repeat them to yourself at various times throughout the day, especially in the moments when you feel as though you are about to give your power away.

Be strong in your truths, and never let anyone tell you who you are!

Believe that you have what you need within you to achieve your goals. The more you believe your affirmation, the stronger you will become.

CHAPTER 18

OWN YOUR LIFE

The greatest glory in living lies not in never falling, but in rising every time we fall.

- RALPH WALDO EMERSON –

* * *

It is important that no matter what is happening in our lives that we make an effort to get up, get dressed, and keep moving forward. Yes, sometimes the issues that we have to deal with may require us to take some downtime, and it is critical that we do so, especially during a crisis. However, at some point, it is imperative that we get our lives back on track.

• •

Make an effort to get up, get dressed, and keep moving forward!

• •

*

One of my grandmother's many sayings were *"nothing tried, nothing done."* When I was growing up, I didn't fully understand what she meant, but as I grew older, I realized that what she meant was: ***if you don't try to do something, you won't accomplish anything***.

Today, this makes perfect sense to me. Sam Walton, the founder of Wal-Mart was laughed at by others when he told them that he'd open a chain of stores in small rural communities and that these stores would be bigger and better than JCPenney's. Many doubted him, but Sam persisted and went ahead with his plans for the Wal-Mart stores. He became highly successful in this endeavor. The fact the Wal-Mart stores are still thriving is a testament to the strong foundation Sam built. **What a vision!**

Believe that you have the power to create your own reality and that some things are worth going the extra mile.

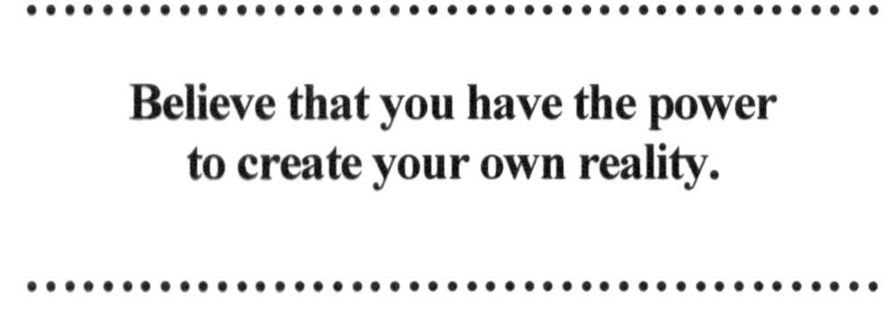

**Believe that you have the power
to create your own reality.**

*

YOU ARE THE BOSS

Barbara Corcoran is someone who didn't know that she would become super successful in real estate or that her career would lead her to become a big part of the TV show *Shark Tank*. Barbara's ex-boyfriend's parting words to her when she had found enough courage to end their business partnership after he had married their secretary was "you'll never survive without me." Barbara has said that since then every time she was thinking of giving up she'd think of something else to do, just because she didn't want them (ex-boyfriend and ex-secretary) to laugh at her. The ex-boyfriend's stinging words reminded her to keep moving forward, no matter what. She called this "the best insurance policy she's ever got." I guess this is when that "I'll show you" mentality will kick in.

Barbara became super successful in real estate and has since written several books, including her bestseller, *Shark Tales: How I Turned $1,000 into a Billion Dollar Business*. This $1,000 was the monies she had borrowed from her ex to start her real estate business. As a Shark member, Barbara has invested in more than twenty-two businesses and is reported to have a net worth of $80 million dollars.

Barbara's story can remind us to keep moving, even when the odds are stacked against us. If we remain focused on our intentions and pay close attention to our attitudes, beliefs, and actions, we can indeed succeed.

If they think you can't, well, just show them that you can. Prove them wrong!

*

As I strive to make progressive changes to the next stages of my life, some things and people will have to become new, and the old will have to go. I've realized now more than ever that if we want to see a different outcome, we have to do things differently, and this includes some of my relationships that I once valued!

There are too many people in our world who are developing too much of the "me, myself, and I" mentality, and it's making me sad (and sick). I think we should find a new word to describe people who are incredibly selfish and who seem to have a short memory.

Yes, I get that everyone's lives are crazy and hectic. It is something that I wrote about extensively in my previous book, and, as I noted there, because we are so busy, we often feel stressed and overwhelmed. But come on: do we have to be selfish all the time? Can we not stop from time to time to give back to our friends, family, and communities (especially when they have asked or begged for our help and support)? I know that I'm not the only one feeling this way (I've been hearing similar complaints from the media and others around me.).

Perhaps, you're feeling this way about the others in your circle right at this moment, or maybe after reading this you may recognize that you could do more to help the people around you.

*

THE "ME, ME" ATTITUDE

The millennials get accused of being selfish and irresponsible, and some are. But they are not the only ones. This "me, me" attitude is creeping up into the older generation too, I'm afraid. Why is this happening? Is this just a North American attitude or is this a global thing?

I believe that at some times it will take a village to get things done. I was brought up the old-fashioned way—to help out in any way I can when the need arises. In many cases, this is not a lot to ask.

We can give some of our time or offer a kind word of encouragement when and where it's required—in the grand scheme of things, it's not that much to give. What do you think?

To make my point, here is an example: Not too long ago, I asked a group of people in my circle, who shall remain nameless, to assist me with a special project I was working on—this was a big deal for me, and I made it clear that it was important. I also made several requests and sent out reminders. Some people went way above and beyond to assist me. And sadly, some said they would, but didn't follow through. The truth is, the ones that I thought would bend over backward to help me mainly because I'd given so much of myself to them over the years didn't do what I had asked of them.

I'm more than okay with having a smaller circle of people around me. Apparently, it's better to have a handful of quality people around you rather than a multitude of selfish, good-for-nothing ones.

What do you think?

I have a huge problem with people who make promises and then don't keep them. It's important to build and maintain credibility. If you're asked to do something and you cannot do it, just say so, and if you decide that you're going to do something for someone, be sure to do it properly—it's okay to throw a little bit of yourself into it. And this is worse: Do not tell someone that everything looks fine, when you obviously don't know because you didn't do what you said you were going to do. Always remember that your word is your bond.

Once again, I will compromise to a certain degree, but I will not conform (I will be shaken, but I will not be moved.). I will not try to change the person who God created me to be just so I can fit in.

I will always strive to become the highest version of myself because I believe there is still room for improvement. What I will <u>NOT</u> do, however, is shrink and play small so others may "look good."

As you look ahead, never forget that someone helped you, and if you find yourself moving onward and upward, at least do your part to help pave the way for someone else. I *really* believe in the "each one, teach one" way of thinking.

And so, I'll leave you with this: How much are you willing to conform? Are you going to strive to do what is right and just? Are you ready to start playing bigger, and will you keep aiming to become a better version of yourself?

*

LIVING WITH HONESTY AND INTEGRITY

I cannot stress how important it is that we strive to live a life of truth, honesty, and integrity. These are some of the characteristics that set successful people apart from the unsuccessful ones. You won't get too far in life if people around you have to wonder whether they can trust you.

If you should find yourself heading in the wrong direction, get off that path and find the right one to trudge on. **Stand in, with, and for the truth!**

*

PRACTICE HUMILITY

There is nothing more fascinating than meeting successful people who remain humble. They think of themselves as merely ordinary people and don't let their status affect the way they live or how they treat others.

Humble people don't mind taking a back seat to let others shine sometimes. They are confident and often possess tremendous inner strength. Most importantly, humble people never forget where they came from.

Mother Teresa said: "If you are discouraged it is a sign of pride, because it shows you trust in your own powers. Never bother about other people's opinion. Be humble and you will never be disturbed."

This may explain the peacefulness that often surrounds humble people.

When I think about humility, I think of people like Bill Gates, Warren Buffet, and Mark Zuckerberg—rich and powerful, yet they look and act like simple everyday people.

Dave Packard, one of the founders of Hewlett-Packard, was also an example of a humble man. Before his death in 1996, he lived in the same small house that he and his wife had built in 1957. He had no material symbols that would indicate he was a billionaire. Upon his death, his family created a eulogy pamphlet with a photo of him sitting on a tractor in farming clothes. The caption made no reference to his association with Hewlett-Packard. Dave Packard bequeathed his 5.6-billion-dollar estates to a charitable foundation upon his death.

I believe humility will carry us a greater distance. Let our work and how we live make all the noise.

How we treat others *truly* says a lot about us.

CHAPTER 19

A NEW PERSPECTIVE

Virtually nothing is impossible in this world if you just put your mind to it and maintain a positive attitude.

- LOU HOLTZ -

* * *

Always aim to look on the brighter side of things. Sometimes just having the ability to change our perspective can allow us to move on to become more productive. When we constantly compare ourselves with others who are perceived to be doing better than we are, we'll rob ourselves of love, joy, and peace.

*

CONSISTENCY IS CRITICAL

In anything we do, consistency is critical, the more consistent we are, the easier things will become. If you consider doing something as simple as baking, cooking, or even learning to drive a vehicle, the more you do it, the better and more comfortable you'll become. If you cook a dish multiple times, for example, you're more likely to remember all the ingredients and the quantities you need to use to get a similar result as last time. It's the same with driving; the first few times can be nerve-wracking, but the more you drive, the more comfortable you'll become. Before long, you'll have no problem driving long distances.

Let's look at consistency on a more serious note. If you talk to the majority of successful people, they'll tell you that consistency is critical to their success. They think and do things differently. Many of them have certain habits and routines that they perform daily. These habits and rituals are ingrained in their minds to the point where they could perform some activities blind folded.

*

FORGIVE YOURSELF FOR PAST MISTAKES AND FAILURES

Forgive yourself for any past mistakes or failures. Use them as opportunity for growth. There is a saying: "The only time you should ever look back is to see how far you've come."

Sometimes it can be difficult to let go of the past, but it is important that we're never held prisoner to it. Everyone has made mistakes, and as Albert Einstein said: *"Anyone who has never made a mistake has never tried anything new."*

Perhaps you have made mistakes in your past that you haven't been able to let go. Know that if you are to forge ahead in any meaningful way it is important that you let go of anything or anyone who has caused you pain. Focus on the positives and continue to do the things that will move you forward. If applicable, work on any bad attitudes, behaviors, beliefs, or actions that may hinder you from creating the life you desire.

If indeed you have made mistakes or have regrets for things you may or may not have done in the past, it's time that you stop beating yourself up. Seek to forgive—yourself and others. Believe me, I know this is easier said than done. However, I'd like you to strive to overcome.

May I remind you that many of us have had some regrets over something? We're only human—so whether it's going down the wrong path when we were teenagers—making gigantic fools of ourselves in front of other people—getting ridiculously low grades in school when we clearly could have done better, sucked at our jobs, or experienced epic failure in our marriages, relationships, or businesses, everyone feels regret for something.

Some of us feel like complete failures, even though some of the things we failed at were beyond our control, yet we keep kicking ourselves. If you are still beating yourself up for past failures and mistakes, remember that you can learn, grow, and go up from here.

*

BREATHE IN, EXHALE, AND LET GO!

Give yourself a pat on the back for the things that you've accomplished in the past, and don't dwell on the bad stuff.

Tell yourself that you're **great**! Keep doing and saying things that will help you to feel better about yourself. The more confident you are about yourself and what you can do, the more progress you'll make going forward.

Remember: If you think you can, YOU can!

Small things can lead to bigger and better things. Keep moving onward and upward!

CHAPTER 20

STAYING POSITIVE

Infuse your life with action. Don't wait for it to happen. Make it happen. Make your own future. Make your own hope. Make your own love. And whatever your beliefs, honor your creator, not by passively waiting for grace to come down from upon high, but by doing what you can to make grace happen...yourself, right now.

- BRADLEY WHITFORD -

* * *

The following on staying positive was included in my last book, and, I think it is worth repeating here. It has been slightly modified and should serve as a quick reminder for you to focus on doing the things that make you *feel* better, and will challenge you to *do* better and *live better*:

> There is no question that at certain times it can be a struggle to remain positive when we are in the process of experiencing or making changes, but if we can remain positive while we go through the motions, we'd be able to focus on ensuring the next step we take will improve our lives.

Here are a few ideas that can help you to remain focused and upbeat:

- **Believe in Yourself:** Having confidence in yourself is critical in achieving success. Sometimes it's the "Yes, I can" moments that will give you the willpower to push yourself forward when you need that extra push.

- Ignore your naysayers, doubters, and haters. If you want to do something that you believe is critical to your success, do not hesitate to proceed forward. Remember that anything is possible when you BELIEVE.

- **Hang with Positive People:** Negative people can drag you down, whereas you can learn and grow with dynamic people. Negative and toxic people can affect you spiritually, emotionally, physically and financially. Positive people can elevate your spirit and help you to stay on track with your goals and objectives. I recommend that you spend more time with the latter.

- **Focus on Your Goals:** Never lose track of your goals. Write them down and remember to evaluate them on a weekly or monthly basis. Ensure your goals are S.M.A.R.T. as discussed in Chapter 13.

- When you achieve each goal, add another one to your list. Keep challenging yourself. Believe that you can create the life you want and deserve.

- **Celebrate Your Victories:** Celebrate each goal as you accomplish them. A pat on the back or treating yourself to something special is highly recommended.

- **Stay Focused:** Focus on making the changes you wish to see. Read inspiring books and take advantage of any other opportunities that may help you to do better.

- **Look Outward:** Now may be a good time to do something special for someone else. This special thing could be as simple as giving away some of your time: playing games, going for a long walk, or taking that person out for a nice lunch or dinner. You might be amazed at how gratifying this simple act can be.

- **Inspire Someone:** Reach out to at least one person daily. Make a phone call. Talk, smile, or nod to the people you meet while you're out and about. Reaching out could make a difference in your life as well as the other party's life.

- **Be Open:** Being open to new adventures and experiences will make your life more enjoyable and meaningful.

- **Observe and Enjoy Nature:** When was the last time you spent some time at a park or took a walk along a beach or a scenic pathway?

- **Listen to Music:** Play the type of music that brings back happy memories. Don't be afraid to listen to your favorite songs again and again. Pretend that no one is listening even if someone is. Learn to be the boss of your own life!

- **Meditate:** Relax and reflect on positive thoughts. Read the *Bible* and other inspiring books on a daily basis. The *Bible* is a great resource for you to find answers that you might be seeking.

- **Keep a Daily Journal:** Use a journal to write down your thoughts and the feelings you are experiencing each day.

- **Practice an Attitude of Gratitude:** It is important that you take some time to write down or make a mental note of all the things you feel grateful for each day. Make time to revisit what you've written on a weekly basis so that you can see your progress.

- **Give Yourself a Gift:** How about treating yourself to something special? A special treat could include a massage, a professional manicure, or a pedicure.

- **Think Happy Thoughts:** When you begin to feel lost and alone, remember the happy moments that you have had in the past. Concentrate on those. Below are a few suggestions to get you to focus on more happy thoughts:

    o Envision yourself taking a hot shower after a long day at work—feel the water running down your back? Think about carving out some time to do this.

o   Envision yourself turning on the music at home—softly—and curling up on the sofa or in bed to read a great book or flip through a magazine. Now, this is something to look forward to.

o   Envision yourself walking into your home and seeing someone, perhaps a spouse or a parent, preparing a lovely dinner, which consists of some of your favorite foods. What emotions are you experiencing? Does this thought bring a smile to your face?

o   Envision yourself on your last getaway. The one where you spent time relaxing in front of the fireplace in the hotel lobby or, better yet, in your room. Did you have room service? How about the lovely lunch or dinner you had when you were away? Did you enjoy your drinks? Did you go dancing after dinner? How was the music?

o   Envision yourself listening to your favorite song on the radio. What feelings are evoked when you hear it? If you were by yourself, would you sing and dance?

Why don't you hum your favorite song (softly if you have to), while you are at work? Again, who cares?

o   How about the last engaging conversation you had? Can you remember a conversation that left you feeling alive and grateful to be present in the moment?

o   Envision yourself holding hands with someone you love—feel the strength in the hand of the love of your life or the tenderness of a child's tiny fingers, entwined with yours.

o   Think about the expression on a loved one's face as he or she opens a gift you gave them. Imagine that he or she loves this gift.

o   Envision yourself watching some kids play. Better yet, can you think of some cute things your kid said or did? Here is an example: A former coworker told me that when her son was around three years old and she would try to discipline him for misbehaving, he would hold his chest and say "Mom, you hurt my heart." When she told me this, it brought tears of laughter to my eyes. We both had a good laugh!

o   Think about the last happy family vacation you took.

o   Think back to the last time you laughed hard and try to re-live that moment.

The above should give you a good start on developing ways to remain positive as you move forward. Feel free to add to this list as you move along.

CHAPTER 21

CONCLUSION

Work hard for what you want because it won't come to you without a fight. You have to be strong and courageous and know that you can do anything you put your mind to.

- LEAH LABELLE -

* * *

As I come to the conclusion of this book, I'd like you to remember that if you think you can, YOU can. *Do not be afraid. Stop doubting, stop worrying, and start BELIEVING in your future!* Envision a life filled with possibilities.

Keep dreaming. Keep believing. Keep trusting, and keep moving forward, no matter what!

If you strongly feel that you should pursue a dream or an opportunity and you begin to doubt yourself or your capabilities, or if you find yourself worrying about how you're going to achieve what you're setting out to do, I'd like you to think long and hard about it. If you choose to go after what it is you desire, be sure to make a strong decision, and then step forward and don't look back.

I want you to give "this thing" everything you've got. Start where you're at, and use what you have. You can use the

Start with 10 Success Blueprint that I shared with you earlier to help you to find and maintain some momentum.

Forget about your past mistakes and failures. If you have failed or have made mistakes in the past, do not let those prevent you from moving forward. Know that yesterday is gone and today is now—live it, feel it, and love it. Tomorrow is a brand-new day that will provide you with an opportunity to begin again, stronger and wiser.

If tomorrow doesn't turn out the way you want it to, still live it, feel it, and love it because it too shall pass.

If you are still breathing, appreciate where you're at. Keep striving to design the life of your dreams.

Never, ever forget where you're coming from, because if you do, you will never know when you arrive at your *sweet* spot.

Do not be afraid to confront and acknowledge your weaknesses. Work to improve them, but remember, you don't have to strive for perfection; just focus on doing the best you can. Try to do your best in all your endeavors.

Never be afraid to face your truths. It is only when you face the truth that you can begin to fix what isn't right and start living a productive, fulfilled, and meaningful life.

Stay upbeat. Don't worry about the little things in life, because it's the big things that really matter. The big things are the ones that will make a difference in your life and in the lives of others.

Set and stick to your goals! You can achieve a high level of success by focusing on your daily intentions, activities, behaviors, and habits, while you navigate your way through your career or business, your finances, relationships, and health.

Never be afraid to leave your comfort zone to go after what you want in life. Know that if you're going to change your life significantly the things you'll require to do so will be outside of your comfort zone. Go out and get them!

Remember that you can take the path less traveled. You may discover many wonders and opportunities along a route that is less traveled.

Stick with positive people. Cut the toxic ones from your life. This is especially important if you are suffering from an addiction or if others are causing you to feel "less than." Remember that we're all diamonds in the rough. A few more scrubs and polishing will have us looking shiny and new.

Keep growing to become the person you want to be. Do not shrink so that other people can feel better about themselves, and do not conform to an image that others think you ought to have. Just be true to yourself.

Stand tall. Keep your shoulders straight! Never stoop to the same levels of negative and toxic people, and do not let anyone "label" you. Know who you are. Discard the lies and own your truths. Strive to raise yourself above any negativity.

Live your life standing up. Do not take things sitting down. When you stand up, you will be able to see things from afar. Strive to live your life with truth, honesty and integrity, and if you should find yourself heading in the wrong direction, get off that path, find the right one, and continue to trudge along.

Be kind. Stop from time to time and lend a helping hand to people, things, and causes. I know that I've told you to focus on *your* dreams and goals. However, it is important that you lift your head up from time to time to help and support others. Sometimes when we take a break from our lives, we may find solutions to our problems or we may find that a way opens up for us that others have created just because we reached out—this might not have happened if we weren't connected, somewhere, somehow. Just remember that there is a balance to everything. At times, you'll need to remain focused on your activities and intentions, and at other times, you'll be required to give to others.

Be humble because humility will carry you a greater distance. Learn to understand and forgive others.

Be grateful. Remember that the little blessings are just as important as the big ones, so honor them!

Remember that the Universe supports you. You can take comfort in knowing that God is with you and fighting for you. He will open the doors *YOU* knock on, so keep knocking. Sometimes our timing might be different from his, but he is usually working for us lovingly, silently, and diligently, and through him, anything is possible. **You don't have to rely on just your strength.**

Keep your eyes on the prize, and learn to walk in YOUR greatness—own it!

Keep doing what is necessary to take your life from where you are to where you want to go.

ALWAYS REMEMBER:

If you think you can, YOU can!

NEVER FORGET THAT YOU CAN START DESIGNING THE LIFE YOU DESIRE, AT ANY MOMENT ON ANY GIVEN DAY.

Dear Reader, thank you so much for reading this book. The fact that you choose this book to read means a lot to me, and I hope that the information contained within will help you to continue to create the life you've always wanted, no matter what. I believe that we can create our own reality!

We can make positive changes in our lives by focusing on our goals and practicing to live each day with intention, passion, and conviction.

I wish you the best in all your endeavors.

Onward and upward!

*

Please help me to impact many more lives. If you enjoyed reading *If You Think You Can, YOU Can,* I'd appreciate if you'd take a moment to leave a review at your favorite online retailer.

Dona M. Deane

Let's stay connected. Join my mailing list at www.donamdeane.com to receive updates and information on the release of my next books.

You can also connect with me via:
Twitter: www.twitter.com/donadeane
LinkedIn: www.linkedin.com/donadeane

NOTES & SUGGESTED READING

Below are some of my favorite books that I highly recommend, depending on the things that pique your interest or the ones that might apply to the areas in which you seek to improve. A lot of knowledge, wisdom, and understanding can be gained simply by reading great books. If you wish to keep learning and growing, it is critical that you keep reading. I will continue to update this list, so be sure to visit my website at www.donamdeane.com

- *Braving the Wilderness: The Quest for True Belonging and the Courage to Stand Alone,* Brene Brown (published by Random House, copyright © 2017).

  In this book, Brown argues that we're experiencing a spiritual crisis of disconnection, and introduces four practices of true belonging that challenge everything we believe about ourselves and each other. She writes "True belonging requires us to believe in and belong to ourselves so fully that we can find sacredness both in being a part of something and in standing alone when necessary. But in a culture that's rife with perfectionism and pleasing, and with the erosion of civility, it's easy to stay quiet, hide in our ideological bunkers, or fit in rather than show up as our true selves and brave the wilderness of uncertainty and criticism."

  www.brenebrown.com

- *Abundance Now: Amplify Your Life & Achieve Prosperity Today,* Lisa Nichols and Janet Switzer (published by Dey Street Books, copyright © 2016).

  In this book, Nichols shares her secrets to creating a life that is rich in every way possible. Focusing on the four areas of life that must be refined to bring true abundance or the 4E's—Enrichment, Enchantment, Engagement, Endowment—Nichols identifies the framework upon which a fulfilled existence is built. *Abundance Now* offers provocative lessons, actionable plans, and real-life case-studies and makes clear what we must do every day to attract abundance, how to act as if we are already living abundant lives, and how to open the door to a life of richness in our work, our relationships, our finances, and in our view of ourselves.

  www.abundancenowonline.com

- *It's All Up to YOU: Strive to Feel Better, Do Better, and Live Better,* Dona M. Deane (copyright © 2017).

  This book will remind you that it's never too late to start making positive changes in your life. Discover how to recognize and deal with the emotions that might be preventing you from living your best life. You'll also learn how to set realistic goals and objectives by focusing on your attitudes, habits, actions, and behaviors. In his book, I shared some of my personal life experiences, as well as the stories of super successful and extraordinary people to inspire and empower you to get up and get moving, no matter what stage in life you're at.

www.donamdeane.com

- *The Success Principles: How to Get from Where You Are to Where You Want to Be,* Jack Canfield (published by HarperCollins Publishers, copyright © 2005).

  This book will teach you how to increase confidence, tackle daily challenges, live with passion and purpose, and realize all your ambitions. Not merely a collection of good ideas, this book spells out the sixty-four timeless principles used by successful men and women through history. Though I haven't read this book in its entirety, I found it extremely valuable. If you want to learn how to set and measure your goals, be sure to read this one.

  www.thesuccessprinciples.com

- *Heart of the Soul: Emotional Awareness*, Linda Francis and Gary Zukav (published by Simon & Schuster, copyright © 2001).

  This book provides help in developing a new emotional awareness that is central to our spiritual development. It explains how the expansion of human perception beyond the five senses leads to a new understanding of power as the alignment of the personality with the soul— "authentic power."

www.zukav.com

- *The Mind of the Soul: Responsible Choice*, Linda Francis and Gary Zukav (published by Simon & Schuster, copyright © 2003).

This book shows you how to take responsibility for the choices you make and break free from illusion that you are a victim of your circumstances. *The Mind of the Soul* describes how each moment in life is a moment of decision. I love this book!

www.zukav.com

- *The Purpose Driven Life*, Rick Warren (published by Zondervan, copyright © 2002).

This book is a guide to a forty-day spiritual journey that will enable you to discover the answers to life's most important question: What on earth am I here for? This book allowed me to discover and understand what my purpose is in a way that no other book that I've read has. I bought a copy of this book around 2006 when I was trying to figure out why I wasn't feeling happy and fulfilled. After reading this book, I realized that there is truth to understanding and continuing to do the things that are aligned with our real life purposes.

www.pastorrick.com

- *The Principles and POWER of VISION*, Dr. Myles Munroe (published by Whitaker House, copyright © 2003)

  In this book, Dr. Munroe will help you capture and fulfill your vision—to transform followers into leaders and the maximization of individual potential—within them. This book will inspire, motivate, and encourage you to start living the life you were created for.

- *Bad Childhood - Good Life,* Dr. Laura Schlessinger (published by HarperCollins Publishers Inc., copyright © 2006)

  In this book, Dr. Laura wrote about the early family dynamics and experiences and our current attitudes and decisions and how our histories impact our adult lives— our choices in people, repetitive situations, and decisions.

www.drlaura.com

- *Human Moments: How to Find Meaning and Love in Your Everyday Life*, Edward M. Hallowell, MD (published by Health Communications, Inc., copyright © 2001)

  This book is about the human moments—the most reliable places to find human moments are in the connections we make, the connection of our hearts, the people and the places that we love.

www.drhallowell.com

- *Life Makeovers*, Cheryl Richardson (published by Broadway Books, a division of Random House Inc., copyright © 2000)

This book is about how tough it is to juggle the daily demands of living in a fast-paced world, and how we can become disconnected from our true selves and what make us happy. It shows how making small changes, over time, can have a huge impact on the quality of our lives.

www.cherylrichardson.com

- *Rich Dad Poor Dad: What the Rich Teach Their Kids About Money – That The Poor And Middle Class Do Not!* Robert Kiyosaki (published by Plata Publishing, LLC, copyright © 2011)

In this book, Robert Kiyosaki shares the story of his two dads, his real father (his poor dad) and the father of his best friend, who became his mentor and his "rich" dad. One man was well educated and remained an employee all his life and the other was "street smart" and an entrepreneur who became one of the wealthiest men in Hawaii. Robert's poor dad struggled financially all his life, but his rich dad didn't. The two dads had different point of views on money, investing, and employment. These two different views shaped Robert's thinking about money.

www.richdad.com

- *The Secret of the Millionaire Mind: Mastering the Inner Game of Wealth*, T. Harv Eker (published by Harper Business, copyright © 2005)

  This book is about the human moments—the most reliable places to find human moments are in the connections we make, the connection of our hearts; the people and the places that we love.

www.harveker.com

- *Feel The Fear ... and Do It Anyway*, Susan Jeffers, Ph.D. (published by Harcourt Brace Jovanovich, Inc., copyright © 1987, 2007)

  This is a guide to self-empowerment. Dr. Susan Jeffers inspires us with dynamic techniques and profound concepts that have helped countless people around the world to learn how to deal with their fears and how to create more meaning in our lives. This book helps us to recognize what we're afraid of, and why and how we can move from victim to creator. In this book, Dr.

Jeffers was not afraid to show her vulnerability with her readers. She wrote in an authentic and caring manner.

www.susanjeffers.com

- *Fear and Other Uninvited Guests,* Harriet Lerner, Ph.D. (published by HarperCollins Publishers Inc., copyright © 2004)

Harriet promises that her book will help people look fear full in the face, challenging readers to consider this difficult emotion as both obstacle and friend. This book is highly recommended for those who wish to understand and conquer their fears.

www.harrietlerner.com

ACKNOWLEDGMENT

I'd like to take this opportunity to acknowledge my husband, Art for allowing me the space I needed to focus on my writing goal. A big thank you!

To my Mom, Geveta and my Dad, Alphonso. Thank you for the patience, generosity, and support you have shown me throughout the years. Mom, you are my rock. I could always count on you to be there whenever I needed you!

To my editor, Kelly Hartigan, for her patience, valuable feedback, and comments during the writing and editing process. I am forever grateful. Kelly, you are a professional!

To my cover designer, Judy Bullard, for her patience, professionalism, and prompt responses to the many changes I requested. Judy you did a fabulous job!

To my amazing book designer, Brenda Van Niekerk, for her patience and professionalism in ensuring both eBook and print copy were of utmost quality. Thank you, again!

To all other family members and friends (too many to count) who have supported me throughout the years. I'm sure you know who you are! Thank you so much for your love and support.

And finally, to all my social media friends and online supporters. Thank you for sharing and supporting my work. I'm forever grateful. You are the best!

ABOUT THE AUTHOR

Dona is an author and entrepreneur who lives in Canada with her husband and two children. She strives to celebrate and enjoy life's simple pleasures and aims to inspire others to live their best lives.

Imagine, believe, trust, and keep moving forward, no matter what challenges you may face along your life's journey has become one of the author's philosophies.

Dona's books are written from the perspective of someone who has worn many shoes: executive, entrepreneur, wife, and mother, among other roles.

She is passionate about happiness, perseverance, and success. Dona has spent countless hours (since 2006), researching and writing about human emotions and changes. She is on a mission to remind others to keep pursuing their goals and dreams, no matter what—it's never too late to get back on track to designing the lives they had envisioned for themselves all along.

Oh, and just one more thing: Dona cannot seem to stop writing since she wrote and published her second book, *It's*

www.ingramcontent.com/pod-product-compliance
Lightning Source LLC
Chambersburg PA
CBHW032025050726
47590CB00006B/2306